Fidget to Focus

Fidget to Focus

Outwit Your Boredom: Sensory Strategies for Living with ADD

Roland Rotz, Ph.D.
Sarah D. Wright, M.S., A.C.T.

iUniverse, Inc.
New York Bloomington

iUniverse books may be ordered through booksellers or by contacting:

iUniverse
1663 Liberty Drive
Bloomington, IN 47403
www.iuniverse.com
1-800-Authors (1-800-288-4677)

Because of the dynamic nature of the Internet, any Web addresses or links contained in this book may have changed since publication and may no longer be valid. The views expressed in this work are solely those of the author and do not necessarily reflect the views of the publisher, and the publisher hereby disclaims any responsibility for them.

ISBN: 978-0-595-35010-0 (sc)
ISBN: 978-0-595-79715-8 (ebook)

Printed in the United States of America

iUniverse rev. date: 11/20/09

Contents

Dedication

This book is dedicated to all members of ADD support groups everywhere. As you sought help to clear the confusion of your life, you searched for information, understanding, and support. Yet *you* are the experts! As you shared the tip or strategy that gets you through the day, without realizing it, you provided help desperately needed by another person in the room. Your creativity, passion, and commitment to improving your lives have challenged the status quo on all levels. Your innovative ideas have sparked change in our knowledge, in our education and training models, in our work and play environments, and even in our government. Perhaps most importantly, your strategies have effected change in yourselves, your children, and the people sitting across the room.

This book could not have been written without you.

Thank you!

Acknowledgments

Fidget to Focus was born years ago and nurtured through the loving care of several key people. I will forever be indebted to these dear friends and colleagues. Thanks to Mark Katz and Terri Fong for showing me how to listen beyond the words and how to think between the lines. When I struggled, you always believed in me. "No judgments" has been and will forever be my New Year's resolution too. Andrea Little Betts, Amy Ellis, and Tiffany Hild—each of you encouraged, supported, and challenged me to take this idea to the next level. Each of you has a part in bringing this book to life. Thank you for your many contributions. Brenda Smith, for your strength to see what others could not and your courage to share even though others may not hear, I thank you for trusting me to share your story so others can find the same hope that I saw in you.

Thanks to my wife, Jody, and my twin daughters, Lindy and Cate, for their love, patience, and understanding for the hours spent away from home while writing *Fidget to Focus*.

Finally, to my co-author, friend, and coach, Sarah Wright, you have accomplished what no one has done before, the writing of *Fidget to Focus*. Believe me, others have tried. I am forever grateful for your passion, your compassion, and your commitment to excellence. This book would not have been written without you.

Roland Rotz, Ph.D.

A conversation with a stranger in a coffee house introduced me to the field of sensory integration. I will always be grateful to Dr. Sarah Turner-Froese for that pivotal moment, for her caring, and for her continuing support.

I thank my clients, friends, and family with whom I have since shared these ideas, and who in turn shared their experiences with me. Many of your stories have made it into this book, and they will go on to inspire others.

My love and thanks to my husband, Christopher, and my children, Becky and Danny, for their support in all things, and to my son for helping to bring me to this calling.

And finally, I want to thank my co-author and friend, Roland Rotz. *Fidget to Focus* is his creation. Without his curiosity to notice and pursue this phenomenon, and his humanity to share what he learned, so many of us would still be struggling to cope, or be embarrassed by our fidgety coping mechanisms. He is a gentle and generous man, and this collaboration has been a great joy to me.

Sarah D. Wright, M.S., A.C.T.

And last but not least, we would both like to thank our publicist and mentor, Penny Sansevieri, our wonderful editor, Melanie Rigney, and our awesome graphic designers at Image Net. Their expertise helped squire this project along, and they took care of details so that we didn't have to.

Roland Rotz, Ph.D., and Sarah Wright, M.S., A.C.T.

Epigraph

"There are only two things I have ever done well: paint and fidget!"

Claude Monet

Preface

Living with Attention Deficit Disorder (ADD) means always looking for a new or different way to manage the ongoing struggles of life. Often it seems that just as we start to get ahead, something is there to trip us up. ADD can make us feel that no matter how hard we try, our lives are and will always be two steps forward and three steps back.

When this derailment happens, there is always someone with the best of intentions, be it a friend, family member, colleague, support group member, coach, or therapist, who will suggest yet another strategy for us to try. And maybe we do try it, hoping that *this* one will work. After all, it works for everyone else. If we live with ADD, we've probably noticed that just about anything will work. But only briefly. Then it all falls apart again. When we experience this kind of failure again and again and again, it is painful, discouraging, and demoralizing.

Every once in a great while, a new idea surfaces that challenges our assumptions about why we do what we do. Such ideas have surfaced on several occasions in the world of ADD. For instance, it would seem obvious that hyperactivity is the result of too much activity in the brain, yet we have learned that hyperactivity is really about *inactivity* in the brain. We also used to think that ADD was a childhood disorder, yet we have learned that many do not outgrow ADD, that it can persist into the teenage years and even into adulthood.

We hope that the ideas in this book will challenge yet more assumptions about why we do what we do. We hope it will give everyone, not just those with ADD, coping strategies that will work, not just briefly, but for a lifetime.

Roland Rotz, Ph.D.
Sarah D. Wright, M.S., A.C.T.
May 2005

CHAPTER 1

Paradigm Shift

Playing Nintendo

For us, the idea started years ago with a story that sparked interest and hope. The story was told by a bright, accomplished, engaging woman with an advanced degree in social work; a bright, accomplished, engaging woman who also has dyslexia and Attention Deficit Disorder (ADD). This is the story she told.

While she was in graduate school, her reading load was extensive. Because she struggles with reading comprehension and working memory, she would have to read passages over and over again before she could understand and remember the material. It would take her *months* to get through a textbook, and there were many of them. Using audio books in some cases helped a little, but she still averaged about two months to finish listening to one book.

In her efforts to get through the texts, she was wearing out her recorder's rewind button. She found that whenever she settled down to listen, her mind would begin to wander. One evening, after rewinding the tape a hundred times, she got tired of trying again and again and again. Frustrated, she decided to take a break and play Nintendo, a game she found mildly challenging, relaxing, and fun.

Feeling guilty, knowing she still had so much work to do, she decided to try playing the game and listening to the tape at the same time. After all, she often found herself doing five things at once! She turned off the game sound; turned on the book tape; and, with her hands on the controls and her eyes glued to her television set, began playing Nintendo while listening to her book. To her surprise, she noticed it was much easier to pay attention to what she was hearing and to remember what she heard.

Using this new strategy, she found she was able to complete her books in just two to four *weeks*, not the two or more *months* it had been taking. In general, she found that she could focus on her tedious reading as long as she had an interesting and stimulating activity going at the same time.

How counterintuitive to be able to focus better while "goofing off" than when trying to concentrate exclusively on her studies! This was the very opposite of what anyone might expect, certainly the very opposite of what she'd been schooled to do. Although confusing at first, the success of her experience led her to continue to use the strategy and to expand it successfully to other arenas, like doodling while taking notes during lectures.

Other Stories

After hearing this story that confounded all of our expectations, we began to share it with others to see if they had had similar experiences. Stories began surfacing in support groups and in individual sessions. The stories extended the concept of a problematic task from reading to difficulty with almost anything tedious or boring. The strategy of playing a video game was extended to almost any simultaneous sensory experience.

Office personnel with ADD report loving their cordless phones because the technology allows them to pace, which allows them to be more comfortable while listening. Others report doodling masterpieces while on the phone. College students doodle while listening to boring lectures and report that it improves their ability to stay focused. One student called it "listening art," describing his doodles as repetitive and lacking creativity because the doodling is simply a means to stay focused on the lecture.

At Christmas every year, vibrating pillows surface on the shopping channels for that perfect gift to help relax and soothe while you sit. A college student with ADD, who drives many hours to get home for Christmas, reported that he would use the pillow for his back to keep him focused while he drove. He found the rhythmic vibrations, rather than relaxing him, helped keep him alert.

An architect with ADD told the story about how his success had led him to a penthouse office suite with a 180-degree view overlooking San Diego Bay. Unfortunately, it also meant that he spent much less time designing and much more time sitting in management meetings. And he hated it. His success was boring him to death, making a misery of his previously happy life. Rather than leaving the successful company he had created, he did three things to regain control of his life. First, he hired a high-level executive to do his management job. Second, he moved this executive into the penthouse suite with all those wonderful windows with their beautiful and distracting views, and moved himself down the hall to an office with a single smaller window. Finally, recognizing that his best work and his most focused efforts came while he was on his feet (and his least effective times were sitting at his desk!), he built a stand-up desk the length of his new office. He continued to play a pivotal role in his company, meeting just one hour a day with his CEO and happily doing the creative design work he loved and was so good at.

As the people with whom we brought this up, our patients, clients, colleagues, and friends, began paying attention to this idea, parents stopped automatically dismissing their children's claims that they could study better while listening to music. The restless and wiggly foot was no longer seen as intending to interrupt and irritate, but rather to increase focus during class. Stories began surfacing about children unable to sit still through a meal who found standing and swaying gently back and forth allowed them to remain at the table with the family. One mother told the story of how her son's school grades mysteriously improved. The only thing he had changed was that he'd been sneaking his iPod to school and listening to his favorite music during class, hiding his headphones under the hood of his sweatshirt.

One client reported that his nonstop mind was calm and focused as long as he was running. He went on to report that if he ran for more than forty-five minutes, his racing mind would remain focused and calm for at least an hour after running. Another young man found a similar strategy. Once he realized how running enabled him to concentrate, he made the decision to try college again, carefully scheduling his classes so that the hour before was free to run. He then arrived at lectures sweaty, breathless, and able to sit still and pay attention.

Is This You?

Do these stories sound familiar to you? Do you ever wonder... Why can I concentrate better on reading while listening to the radio? Why can I pay attention longer in boring lectures if I'm playing games on my PDA? Why do I feel less restless and more attentive while I'm standing? Why does my concentration improve while I'm chewing gum? Why do I feel at rest while in motion?

If any of this sounds familiar to you, you are not alone. In this book, we will show you why these strategies work, how to determine what your own best strategies are, and how to use them to advantage in all areas of your life.

CHAPTER 2

Current Concept of ADD

Fidgety Phil

Let me see if Philip can
Be a little gentleman
Let me see, if he is able
To sit still for once at table.
Thus Papa bade Phil behave;
And Mamma look'd very grave.
But fidgety Phil,
He won't sit still;
He wriggles
and giggles,
And then, I declare
Swings backwards and forwards
And tilts up his chair,
Just like any rocking horse;
"Philip! I am getting cross!"
See the naughty restless child

Growing still more rude and wild.

Till his chair falls over quite.

Philip screams with all his might.

Catches at the cloth, but then

That makes matters worse again.

Here a knife, and there a fork!

Philip, this is cruel work.

Table all so bare, and ah!

Poor Papa, and poor Mamma

Look quite cross, and wonder how

They shall make their dinner now.

Historical Overview

The poem, "Fidgety Phil," written in 1844 by German physician Heinrich Hoffmann, is the first known description of ADD. Since Dr. Hoffman penned his poem many decades have passed, yet our description of the cluster of symptoms remains essentially the same. In contrast, our understanding of the underlying cause of these behaviors has undergone a notable change. Without going into great detail, we can illustrate this shift simply by reviewing the changes in name applied to this cluster of symptoms in our medical literature over the years.

As early as 1902, the lectures of George Frederic Still to the Royal College of Physicians in England published in the British journal *Lancet*, characterized similar symptoms in children as Morbid Defects of Moral Control. This perspective changed in the 1940s, when several researchers at the Wayne County

Training School in Northville, Michigan, studied the effects of brain injury in a group of mentally retarded children. Among the symptoms observed were distractibility, hyperactivity, and impulsivity. In 1947, their *Psychopathology and Education of the Brain Injured Child* was published, and the symptoms of distractibility, hyperactivity, and impulsivity were defined to be Minimal Brain Damage Syndrome. Then, in 1962, when scientists were unable to associate anatomical brain damage with the symptoms in other children, they renamed it Minimal Brain Dysfunction. A few years later, and congruent with this more neurological explanation, the *Diagnostic and Statistical Manual of Mental Disorders, Second Edition* (DSM-II) in 1968 defined this same cluster of symptoms as Hyperkinetic Syndrome of Childhood.

By 1980, when the DSM-III was first published, the definition of the syndrome had evolved into a more behavioral and descriptive one. The neurological understanding also began to shift from a focus on hyperactivity to a focus on inattention. Thus came about the name Attention Deficit Disorder with and without Hyperactivity. The DSM-III's 1987 revision changed the name again, both to better integrate the hyperactivity aspect and to shorten the name. The syndrome became known as Attention Deficit Hyperactivity Disorder. Finally, the latest revision of the diagnostic manual, DSM-IV, was published with the definitions currently in use. That was in 1994. The syndrome is now called Attention Deficit/Hyperactivity Disorder and includes three subtypes: Predominantly Hyperactive-Impulsive Type, Predominantly Inattentive Type, and Combined Type.

The syndrome itself has thus gone through at least half a dozen and, depending on how we look at it, perhaps as many as twenty-five different names in the past century. These include:

* Morbid Defects of Moral Control
* Minimal Brain Damage Syndrome
* Minimal Brain Dysfunction
* Hyperkinetic Syndrome of Childhood
* Attention Deficit Disorder (ADD)
* Attention Deficit Hyperactivity Disorder (ADHD)
* Attention Deficit/Hyperactivity Disorder (AD/HD)

Current Understanding

The current understanding of ADD suggests that the syndrome is a family of chronic neurobiological disorders that affect our capacity to attend to tasks (inattention), inhibit behavior (impulsivity), and regulate activity level (hyperactivity) in developmentally appropriate ways. These impairments are all in what are termed our executive or higher-level functions, which also include our capacity for planning, sequencing, problem solving, initiation of action, and self-control.

When our executive functions are impaired, our behavior can be affected in the following ways:

* we have trouble staying focused on a task
* we show great initiative, but poor follow-through
* we have poor planning and timing skills
* we are disorganized

* we interrupt in conversations
* we act without thinking
* we have trouble sitting still

While any one of us might have one or all of these troubles at some time in our lives, it is the intensity, duration, and pervasiveness of the symptoms that differentiate ADD. If we have had more of these problems compared with other people our age, and if we've always had them, then ADD is a possibility.

What Else Do We Know about ADD?

Today, we know that ADD first appears in childhood, frequently continues into adolescence, and often persists into adulthood. Current research suggests approximately 3 to 5 percent of school age children have ADD. Some studies suggest even more. We know that ADD exists worldwide and that it has a strong genetic component.

We know that other conditions are often present with ADD, conditions such as depression, anxiety, and learning disabilities. We know that the complications of untreated ADD, particularly when combined with these other conditions, can result in repeated failures in life. Unchecked, this can lead to poor self-esteem, inadequate social skills, behavioral disorders, drug abuse, and addictions, which eventually impact our ability to stay in school, keep a job, or maintain the relationships that are important to us.

Diagnosis and Treatment

Receiving help for ADD means getting an accurate diagnosis and proper follow-up treatment. It is important to first obtain a thorough evaluation and diagnosis from a *knowledgeable professional* familiar with ADD. We emphasize knowledgeable professional because so many conditions have ADD-like symptoms.

This diagnostic process should include a complete history and behavioral observations from several people in different environments. It is important to include the observations of several people, because it is notoriously hard for those of us with ADD to be accurate in our self-observations. Parents and teachers are enlisted to help when evaluating children. Spouses, friends, and co-workers should be enlisted when evaluating adults.

Additional testing may be done to evaluate health, cognitive functioning, and educational achievement level. Educational achievement level and IQ are important when evaluating ADD because the smarter we are, the better we are at compensating, and the better we can hide our struggles. Being good at faking it doesn't mean we don't have ADD. It just means we are spending lots of time and energy compensating for it, time and energy we could be using for other things. Tests for learning disabilities help reveal other hidden struggles that may masquerade as ADD, or that may exacerbate it. Additional health tests are performed to rule out other possible causes of the symptoms such as thyroid problems, sleep apnea, allergies, hormonal imbalances, or other neurological or psychological problems.

The current standard of treatment for ADD is a multimodal approach that includes coaching or counseling, cognitive/behavior therapy, and medication. We all know that coaching, counseling, and therapy happen in an ongoing way over a period of time. What we may not know is that to find the right medication or medications at the right dosages may take several months of monitoring and repeat visits with our doctor. Taking this time to get it right is well worth it, though. It's the difference between having the right eyeglasses prescription and using just any old pair, the difference between seeing really clearly and being able to see only a bit better. Many professionals are also encouraging improved diet and exercise habits, as these have been shown to make a notable improvement in symptoms. This multimodal approach involving medication, counseling of some kind, and lifestyle changes results in the best outcome for most patients.

Review

* Our understanding of the cause of ADD has changed dramatically since the early 1900s.

* Although we still don't know exactly what causes it, we now know that ADD is a neurologically based problem, not a Morbid Defect of Moral Control.

* Current research suggests that 3 to 5 percent of school age children in the United States have ADD.

* Although some problematic behaviors may diminish as a person matures, we now know that ADD first appears in childhood, frequently continues into adolescence, and often persists into adulthood.

* Untreated ADD can lead to poor self-esteem, inadequate social skills, behavioral disorders, drug abuse, and addictions.

* Treatment starts with a thorough diagnosis from a knowledgeable professional familiar with ADD.

* Tests may be performed to rule out other possible causes of the symptoms such as thyroid problems, sleep apnea, allergies, learning disabilities, hormonal imbalances, or other neurological or psychological problems.

* Current treatment involves a multimodal approach that may include coaching or counseling, cognitive or behavior therapy, lifestyle changes, and medication.

CHAPTER 3

A New View of ADD

Advances in Research

Recent research suggests that ADD is a disorder with a signif-icant genetic component. It is perhaps the most inheritable of all psychological or neurological problems. Russell Barkley, one of the best known researchers into the causes and effects of ADD, tells us that if a child has ADD, there is a 15 to 20 percent chance that the mother has or had it and a 25 to 30 percent chance the father has or had it. Further, there is a 25 to 35 percent chance a sibling will also have it.

While geneticists are using advanced techniques to learn more about ADD, neuroscientists are taking advantage of equally notable advancements in their discipline to tremendously expand our understanding of this disorder. New technologies such as electroencephalograms (EEGs), positron emission tomography (PET), single photon emission computed tomography (SPECT), magnetic resonance imaging (MRI), and functional magnetic resonance imaging (fMRI), allow us to noninvasively study the brain. We can now view and measure the morphology, examine the electrical activity, and examine the variable glucose and oxy-gen consumption of different parts of the brain. Some of these technologies take snapshots, but others like fMRI allow viewing the living brain in action.

These tools have allowed us to compare the brains of people with ADD to those of controls in scientifically significant numbers. Perhaps most valuable in the growing scientific literature is the awareness that ADD is not specific to one particular region of the brain. It is seen in dopamine depletions, abnormalities, and disregulation throughout the prefrontal, frontal, striatal, limbic, and basal ganglia regions of the brain. The latter areas are closely connected to the frontal lobes in feedback loops that provide for improved interpretation of sensory input. These five areas together are heavily involved in the control, planning, and execution of complex behaviors such as inhibition, arousal, attention, memory, planning, sequencing, and rhythm. The most recent models that explain ADD use these areas to describe the function of processing sensory input.

The frontal lobe and associated areas of the cortex (the prefrontal and striatal areas) are responsible for executive functioning. These areas are primarily involved in attention to tasks, focus, decision making, planning, memory, restlessness, and inhibition of actions, thoughts, and mood. Underactivity in these areas of the brain leads to disorders of executive functioning, which are often described as trouble with inattention and disinhibition of thoughts, feelings, and behaviors.

The limbic system involves many structures in the brain and is the basis of our primary emotions and drives. If properly regulated, the limbic system provides for normal emotional changes, energy levels, sleep routines, and management of stress. If underactive, we might see (or see what appears to be) a person who is late to react and who has low arousal in mornings, diffi-culty with transitions, and poor stress management.

Finally, situated in the very base of the brain is the reticular activating system, which serves as the attention center of the brain. Receiving information directly from the ascending sensory tracts, it is a complex collection of neurons that brings together signals from the external and internal world. This is the place where our senses come together with thoughts and feelings.

The reticular activating system captures the rhythm of life, projecting it upward to the limbic system and the activity centers of the cortex. This system balances information input for impul-sivity, motor activity, learning, self-control, and motivation. If functioning normally, it provides the neural connections to be interested, to be motivated, and to pay attention to the correct task. Without proper filtering of the reticular activating system, one would experience a high level of attraction to all parts of the sensory input, whether it comes from external sources or internal sources like thoughts or feelings.

Given our growing understanding of the interplay between the frontal lobes and the reticular activating system, it is no surprise that recent research out of Harvard Medical School suggests that ADD may be caused by a deficiency of the neuro-transmitter norepinephrine in the ascending reticular activation system. Although a lot of media attention has been given to how medications like Ritalin increase the levels of dopamine in the frontal lobe region, it turns out that Ritalin also increases the levels of norepinephrine in this deeper part of the brain.

Review

* We now know that ADD is highly inheritable, the most inheritable of all psychological or neurological problems.

* Recent advances in neuroscience, including the ability to view living brains through various scanning technologies, have greatly increased our understanding of ADD.

* We now know that ADD is a broad-based disregulation affecting the prefrontal, frontal, striatal, limbic, and basal ganglia regions of the brain.

* These areas of the brain interact in feedback loops that provide for improved interpretation of sensory input and are heavily involved in the control, planning and execution of complex behaviors such as inhibition, arousal, attention, memory, planning, sequencing and rhythm.

* We do not know yet what causes ADD but, among other agents, the deficiency and disregulation of the neurotransmitters dopamine and norepinephrine in the frontal region, in the associated regions of the cortex, and in the ascending reticular activation system may play a role.

CHAPTER 4

A Sensory Short Course

What We Can Learn from Goldilocks

Some people love listening to loud music. It makes them feel alive and helps invigorate them. For others, that much sound is overwhelming. They feel assaulted by the music and can't think. These people feel at their best in a quiet environment. Some people love the thrill of speed and like nothing better than to race straight down the hill on their bicycle or skis. Others prefer to walk or to cross-country ski. Some people love their knick-knacks and fill the house with them, each one a treasure with a story attached. Others prefer an uncluttered, almost Zen-like simplicity in their surroundings. Why is that?

We all know the story of "Goldilocks and the Three Bears." Goldilocks didn't like her bed to be too hard or too soft, but just right. She didn't like her porridge too hot or too cold, but just right. What we may not know though, is that *we* are just like Goldilocks. We don't like things in our lives to be too hard or too soft, too hot or too cold. We like to have them just right—just right for *us*. We each have a comfort zone where we feel at our best, neither too loud nor too quiet, neither too frantic nor too bored. This comfort zone is our optimal level of arousal, also called our optimal level of alertness.

If the world around us is too much for our senses to easily cope with, it can be very difficult. There are a number of books in the popular press right now about how overwhelming the world can feel. These include *The Highly Sensitive Person, The Out-of-Sync Child*, and *Too Loud Too Bright Too Fast Too Tight*, to name a few. Knowing about sensory overwhelm and learning there is something we can do about it can be life-changing. But what if, instead of finding much of the world *over*whelming, we find much of it *under*whelming? What do we do then?

The Sluggish Brain

Now that modern technology has allowed us to see the structures, the oxygen and energy consumption, and the electrical activity of our living, functioning brains, we know that one aspect of an ADD brain is that it can run too inefficiently.

Dr. Alan Zemetkin and his team of researchers at the National Institute of Mental Health published a landmark paper in the *New England Journal of Medicine* in November 1990. Using PET scans (positron emission tomography), they found a link between glucose metabolism—the energy used to fuel the brain—and the ability to maintain attention. During a monotonous auditory-attention continuous performance task specifically designed to measure the ability to pay attention over time, they found that the areas of the ADD brain that control attention use less glucose and so are less active than the same areas of the brain in control subjects.

Dr. Daniel Amen's more recent work with single photon emission computed tomography (SPECT) imaging has led him to draw a similar conclusion. He observes that most ADD people have normal activity in their brains while at rest. However, when performing a task that requires concentration, they experience decreased activity in the prefrontal cortex rather than the expected increased activity that is seen in a normal control group. Images that illustrate this phenomenon are accessible on his Web site, www.BrainPlace.com, in the image atlas.

We think the brain of an ADD person is often underactivated or underaroused, a state we think is aptly described as underwhelmed. The particular areas involving activation include in part the right hemisphere, the prefrontal cortex, the basal ganglia, the thalamus, the hippocampus, the locus ceruleus, and the reticular activating system. Each one of these areas plays a critical role in the interpretation, transfer, manipulation, and organization of sensory information in the brain.

From a neurologist's point of view, underarousal is generally considered to be an underrepresentation of critical neurotransmitters that facilitate the transfer of electrical impulses, which in turn represents a thought or action. There continue to be a great deal of questions about how this process really works. However, by watching and learning, we are beginning to understand one very important part of the process: *underarousal seeks arousal*.

There is a homeostasis, a tendency to maintain internal equilibrium, in our neurobiological system that attempts to compensate when we are underaroused. We use our own built-in sensory mechanisms to increase neural stimulation, which, from an ADD perspective, allows us to improve focus. In essence, our distractibility is really attractability to interesting things around us. Our restlessness is not just an expression of trying to "get out the fidgets" in order to become calm. It is rather an attempt to self-arouse to become focused.

OT for the Masses

Most of us have never even heard of occupational therapy (OT). If we have, it has probably been in the context of a disabled child, recuperating accident victim, or stroke patient. This is unfortunate, because the field has a lot to teach us about our normal selves, how and why we do what we do, and how to do it better.

The field of occupational therapy has long been aware of the link between sensory input, behavior, and neural functioning, thanks largely to the work of A. Jean Ayres. Dr. Ayres developed sensory integration theory to give us a better model of the relationship between behavior and brain function. She was particularly interested in the relationship among neural functioning, sensory-motor behavior, and early academic learning. We now know the interplay of sensory-motor behavior and neural functioning extends beyond childhood and affects us all our lives.

Sensory integration theory has led to the concept of optimal arousal. This is the idea that to be able to pay attention and perform a task in a way that is appropriate to a specific situation, our nervous system must also be in state of alertness appropriate for that particular activity. Once we consider that there is an optimal level of arousal, this leads naturally to the concept of self-regulation, the ability to attain, maintain, and change our level of arousal appropriately for a task or situation. Mary Sue Williams and Sherry Shellenberger have created a wonderful program called *How Does Your Engine Run?* to teach self-regulation through sensory-motor stimulation based on these concepts.

When we use the term "sensory-motor", what do we mean? Everyone is aware of the five senses (seeing, hearing, touching, tasting, and smelling) that inform about the world around us. But we may not be as aware of two additional senses that, at an unconscious level, tell us about our own bodies and our relationship to the world. One, the vestibular system, gives us our sense of gravity, balance, rhythm, and motion. It is intimately intertwined with the brain circuitry of the other senses—especially sight, hearing, and touch—and serves as a reference through which all stimuli get processed. The other is the proprioceptive sense that lets us know just how hard our muscles, joints, and tendons are working, and gives us an awareness of body position. The vestibular and proprioceptive senses are intimately involved in all motor activities, so the term "sensory-motor" is the catchall used to refer to all of these senses together. Because the vestibular and proprioceptive senses involve movement and rhythmic activity, they are particularly important in self-regulation.

Evolving Sensory Needs

In the first chapter of *How Does Your Engine Run?*, Williams and Shellenberger give us an overview of what is known about sensory-motor activities and self-regulation. The authors emphasize how every one of us has an innate drive to seek and receive the sensory-motor input our bodies and brains need to develop and function properly. As our nervous systems mature, this inner drive remains, but the need for the degree of intensity, duration, and frequency of sensory motor experiences changes and usually decreases.

By the time we are adults, observes Maryann Trott, author of *Sensibilities*, most of us have discovered the things that help us to achieve and maintain an appropriate state of being for the activities we engage in. If we have been allowed to choose, for the most part we have selected careers, hobbies, and leisure activities that fit our needs. As adults we also usually have the freedom to move around, change tasks, sip drinks, rock or swivel in our chairs, or use the other means to help us stay alert and attend. Children, however, do not always know what they need, and do not have the same freedoms that adults take for granted.

Unfortunately, some adults believe that if children are moving about, they cannot possibly be paying attention. Williams and Shellenberger point out that to the contrary, most children can *either* sit still *or* pay attention. They actually need to move, need to get sensory-motor input, to pay attention. It is really no different for adults. However, the adult's slight movements while sitting and listening are rarely considered rude or a sign of inattention. This is probably because these slight movements are both less obvious than the sensory-motor activities engaged in by children and, because these movements are so universal, they are socially acceptable.

Review

*   We each have a neurological comfort zone, neither over-whelmed nor bored to tears, that allows us to be able to pay attention and perform a task in a way that is appropriate to a specific situation.

*   We can use sensory-motor activities, which affect us neuro-logically, to enter and remain in our optimal zone.

*   In addition to the five senses that inform of the world around us (seeing, hearing, touching, tasting, and smelling), we have two senses (vestibular and proprioceptive) that inform us about our bodies; whether we are moving or upright and how hard our bodies are working. These systems together provide the sensory-motor input that we use to stay in our zone.

*   Everyone has an innate drive to seek and receive the sensory-motor input his or her body and brain needs.

*   Our sensory-motor needs evolve over our lifetimes with regard to intensity, duration, and frequency of sensory-motor experiences.

*   Generally, children need more sensory-motor input—more senses involved, greater intensity, longer duration, and more frequently—than adults do.

*   Underarousal seeks arousal.

CHAPTER 5

Boredom vs. Interest

Boredom

For almost anyone with ADD, there is an underlying and ever present issue of whether an activity is boring or interesting. If something is interesting, it seems we could do it almost forever. When fully engaged, we often forget to eat and easily put off sleep, looking up from our efforts and finding to our surprise that it is dawn. If something is boring, it is very difficult for a person with ADD to do. It may seem to us impossible to persevere in such an activity. Boredom is felt to be the kiss of death. And at some level, it is.

Years ago, miners would take a canary into the mine shaft with them to use as a bad air detector. If the sensitive creature died, it warned the miners to leave before they too succumbed. We believe that to those of us with ADD, boredom is a bit like those canaries. It warns us when there is not enough going on for us to feel alert and "alive." It warns us that our brains are becoming *under*whelmed.

As we mentioned earlier, the reticular activating system captures the rhythm of life, projecting it upward to the limbic system and the activity centers of the cortex. If, during a particular activity, the neural input to the reticular activating system is not sufficient to in turn adequately excite the neurons of the cortex, we experience the activity as boring.

Boredom thus signals disregulation of the coordinated efforts of the cortex, limbic, and reticular activating systems. It is the canary in the mine warning us these systems are not sustaining us well, and that next we can expect to experience learning difficulty, memory impairments, low self-control, poor planning and organizing, and an inability to stay focused on the activity.

If all our neural feedback systems are properly stimulated and active, then focused interest is easily sustained. Many people with ADD understand this intuitively. Frequently, efforts are made to make a task interesting or fun to make it doable at all. Perhaps we choose to use cool paper and new colored pens to write our thank-you letters, or decide we're going to race to see how fast we can finish a chore. As many of us know, finding momentary interest in something is not hard. The difficulty is maintaining the interest through the completion of the task.

It is not uncommon for those of us with ADD to jump into a large project with great excitement. The beginning of a project is a time when there are lots of new ideas, brainstorming is the primary activity, and structure is defined by getting together with others to talk about the new ideas. This part is fun. This part is easy. And to begin with, when there is tremendous interest in and focus on the project, a lot can get done.

Interest equals focus with ADD. Unfortunately, the demands of the project often involve tedious work that requires sustained effort and concentration. Without ways to keep the ideas novel, and with the expectation that we now must follow the well-devised plan developed during the initial planning stage, boredom sets in. At this point there is not enough stimulation, either external or internal, to provide enough of the needed excitement to enable us to remain interested in and focused on the task. It is at this point that we become bored or underwhelmed.

The result of this underwhelm, this neurological understimulation, can literally shut down our prefrontal cortex—our thinking brains. When this happens, we experience the Blank Screen Syndrome. We can't come up with any ideas or think of what to say or what to do. When it is important for us to produce something in which we have no interest, those of us with ADD can experience what feels like cognitive emptiness. It makes us feel stupid. Despite the obvious importance of doing the task, it is nearly impossible to produce anything because we are drawing a complete and utter blank.

Making Things Interesting

Procrastination adds an interesting twist to this dilemma of boredom versus interest. Putting off a large project until the last minute can cause anyone a high level of anxiety and even panic. For many of us with ADD, the state of mind that occurs at midnight when the project is due at 8:00 in the morning becomes the perfect state of being. As the deadline approaches, the adrenalin combines with caffeine (and perhaps endorphins) to produce just the right amount of neural stimulant for us to complete the project with ease, and often with a significant degree of success.

Many students with ADD apply the procrastination method with gusto. Planning and timing skills, which are also impacted by the underactive neural structure, are even less well developed in youngsters than in the scenario we describe above. Because of this, their projects often do not get completed on time. The high school students who ace their exams but get Fs on their homework, and the college students with the half-dozen incompletes, are probably the students with ADD.

A commonly used project-management strategy involves taking a large project and breaking it down into five shorter, supposedly easy-to-complete projects. Unfortunately, for those of us with ADD, this only makes one boring project into five boring projects. Rather than cloning the difficulties, it is more effective for us to create very real, very structured, intermediate project deadlines with a high level of accountability. Without consequences, without a serious need to complete these intermediate deadlines, the tendency for us is to put them off because they are not real anyway.

Another commonly used strategy recommended to us is making a list. Unfortunately, after the first few days when the novelty wears off, making lists also ranks high on the boredom meter. Orderly lists are often substituted with Post-it notes plastered everywhere, or scraps of scribbled paper shoved into every conceivable pocket, notebook, and purse. Some of us find a PDA a sufficiently interesting toy that we can sustain effective use of it over time. The fact that our PDAs often come with amusing but mindless games to play discreetly during meetings also helps.

Seeking interesting and stimulating events or environments crosses into every aspect of our lives. What is boring is watching a single television show. What is interesting is channel surfing while watching three shows simultaneously (and quite successfully). What is boring is sitting down to have a long conversation.

What is interesting is talking and walking along the beach; smelling and listening to the sea; noticing the waves, the birds, and the seashells; and successfully focusing on and enjoying the conversation.

This need to seek interesting and stimulating events even shows up in our relationships. Dr. John Ratey, professor of psychiatry at Harvard Medical School, wrote in *The Foibles, Frailties and Frustrations of Attention* that when ADD is an element in a relationship, there is a tendency to seek out conflict or trauma. For better or worse, when there is conflict in our relationships, it adds spice to our interactions and keeps the relationship interesting.

Attractability

When our ADD brains are understimulated, our neurochemistry becomes disregulated. We suspect that what we experience as boredom or underwhelm is in fact this disregulation in our neurochemistry. In order to compensate for or alleviate this uncomfortable state, our ADD brains naturally seek activation through sensory-motor input. The sensory-motor input ultimately stimulates the frontal lobe, allowing us to focus, plan, and execute activities.

Imagine being required to sit still and read a boring book in your least favorite subject, and imagine you have reread the last page five times and still cannot remember what it said. For those of us with ADD, the boredom of these moments is almost torturous. In this understimulated state of mind, we may appear to an observer to be highly distractible and unable to focus on anything. However, this would be an inaccurate observation, as in this moment we are actually attracted to or paying attention to everything, simultaneously.

Distractibility is really attractability. Our sensory input goes into overtime trying to activate an underactive brain. For some of us, this sensory-motor input may take the form of a wiggly foot or doodling on a scrap of paper. For others, it may be suddenly noticing the familiar sound of Muzak in the background. Still others may find great interest in counting the corners in the ceiling tiles. Some of us may find that this is a time when internal distractions like daydreams or worries engage us. We may even create excitement by tilting our chairs back on two legs and working to stay balanced for seconds at a time.

So why do we wiggle and fidget? Well, obviously, we wiggle and fidget to remove the tedium of the moment. This is true for anyone. However, and more importantly for those of us with ADD brains, the rhythmic simultaneous sensory stimulation of jiggling a foot or doodling takes this process one step further. Because the sensory-motor activity engages our brain, quickly stimulating the frontal lobes, we literally *fidget to focus*!

Review

*   If all neural feedback systems are properly stimulated and active, then focused interest is easily sustained.

*   The underactive or underwhelmed ADD brain is in a state of unrest, which we often experience as boredom.

*   Distractibility is really attractability. This person's sensory input goes into overtime trying to activate an underactive brain. It is attracted to everything at the same time in an effort to achieve this activation.

*   Fidgeting—rhythmic sensory stimulation—is our body's natural way of activating our understimulated brains to facilitate focus, which allows us comfort and rest.

CHAPTER 6

Arousal Strategies

Sensory Arousal Strategies

A nurse with ADD shared the story of the strategy she used to get through her nurse's training. She did just fine in classes or when she was actively involved in something. But as she walked from one activity to another, she would in some sense lose her way. In that lull between activities she would drift off into her own thoughts, begin to worry about this or that, and forget where she was going. Serendipitously, she discovered a perfect strategy using a set of Chinese exercise balls she had. She'd originally used them as a plaything, a finger fidget, but discovered an even better use for them. She explained, "I would just put those in my pocket and it would feel like it would be the thing that would allow me to get from one space to another." Every time she'd take a step, the balls would bang together just very lightly in her pocket and she'd hear these little chimes. It would be that rhythmic auditory input that kept her present and able to get to her next activity on time.

Using sensory stimulation to improve functioning dates back to our earliest civilizations. Whether the goal is to enhance pleasure, increase focus, improve health, or decrease pain, the intent of the sensory activity is to manipulate the body's cognitive, emotional, and behavioral systems in pursuit of that greater state of being.

One of the earliest methods of influencing the body and mind through sensory experience was music—specifically, drumming. Jeff Strong, director of the REI Institute, an organization that focuses on the effects of music on the central nervous system, points out that shamanic and rhythmic drumming date back twenty thousand to thirty thousand years and are considered to be among the oldest methods of healing. The rhythmic patterns are surprisingly similar across continents, languages, cultures, and time. There is hardly a place in this world where rhythm, usually in the form of drumming, hasn't embedded itself into the very fabric of society.

Another ancient and traditional sensory-motor activity to support cognitive function is the use of a chaplet. Using a chaplet, or string of beads, to keep track of prayers began some twenty-five hundred years ago in ancient India. This evolved into the Catholic tradition as a rosary, and into the Middle Eastern tradition as worry beads. As indispensable as chaplets are for counting prayers, undoubtedly the gentle rubbing of the beads as they are held also helps the supplicants stay present and focused in their efforts. In the secular world, the worry beads are a traditional accessory in Greece, helping to while away idle moments or siphon off tension in times of stress.

As we look around, it is not hard to find sensory arousal strategies in use in our modern-day environments. Whether we choose red and chartreuse to paint our fire engines to alert us, or mauve and beige to paint our hospitals to calm us, we use colors to manipulate our senses. We use scented candles and room fresheners to create environments that please and welcome us. We use terry cloth towels after our baths to invigorate us, and soft sheets to soothe us to sleep. We use chewing gum and soda, tea, and coffee to keep us going. And we suffer ubiquitous upbeat Muzak because studies have shown it to increase productivity and moral.

In classrooms we have begun to recognize the importance of multisensory teaching. Not only have we begun to recognize the value of multisensory teaching, but we are beginning to see the subtle variations in each student's sensory needs. A story in the wonderful book *Unicorns Are Real* by Barbara Meister Vitale tells of a teacher who noticed curious inconsistencies in some of her students' abilities. Some were having peculiar troubles with spelling. When they sat at their desks doing a writing assignment or taking a spelling test, they were terrible spellers. But as soon as she said, "Spelling bee contest! We're going to race!" something extraordinary would happen. These same students who couldn't spell sitting down would excitedly jump up, run to the blackboard, write standing up, work fast to compete with the other students, then run to take their seats again. Under this set of conditions, they *could* spell.

When we see a restless child in school, movement strategies often work to "get out the fidgets" and help the student regain his or her alertness comfort zone. This movement may be delivering a note to the office, which gives the child both a brief break from the classroom and a chance to get some exercise. Or, the movement may be as simple as allowing the child to stand instead of sit at his or her desk.

Recess is one of the most effective resources available in school to help restless children re-center and pay attention. Like the men described in the first chapter who found they could sit still and focus after running for an extended interval, a good, hard game of soccer or tag at recess can make all the difference in whether a child will be able to stay on task for the rest of the day.

Non-Sensory Arousal Strategies

Perhaps best known of all the arousal strategies are those that are biochemical in nature and that ultimately affect the way we think, feel, and behave. We drink coffee or tea to wake us up in the morning, to keep us going through the afternoon slump, and to save our bacon when we're working until the wee hours under a deadline. Chocolate is used by many for the same reasons. Stimulants also occur in herbs and spices used in traditional medicines. Ephedra, recently banned as a dietary supplement by the U.S. Food and Drug Administration, is a notorious example. Some common pharmacy medications also have stimulant effects. For example, although drowsiness is a common side effect for most people taking antihistamines, for some these drugs have a paradoxical stimulant effect. Our own bodies produce some well-known stimulants. Long-distance runners often report increased energy and power at some point in a race, a second wind, resulting from the release of endorphins in their brain. And who hasn't experienced a rush of adrenaline at some time in their lives?

After the use of caffeine, however, the most frequently used non-sensory arousal strategies seem to be those that cause us the greatest harm. They are also not necessarily recognized as being, in part, arousal strategies, and are often considered simply to be moral failings, the result of bad upbringing or bad character.

The nicotine from tobacco, while very effective as an arousal strategy, comes with other chemicals that together have a nasty side effect: cancer. Amphetamine-based street drugs are frequently used for their stimulating effect. Because of this effect, combined with very rapid uptake and lack of purity, they are often very toxic and addictive.

Addictions themselves are frequent mechanisms for sensory arousal. Addictions exist not only in the chemical realm, like drug addiction and alcoholism, but also in the behavioral realm. Addictions such as these include computers, food, collecting, shopping, pornography, sex, and gambling. In dealing with an addictive behavior, no matter how motivated we are to overcome that habit, until we find something constructive that gives us the same kick, the same stimulation that the other behavior gives us, it will be very hard to shift.

Many experts have begun to realize that relationship conflict is one of the strategies used by people with ADD. Dr. John Ratey, who is an expert both in aggression and in ADD, talks about the need for conflict and trauma in arenas related to relationships. Dr. Daniel Amen points out that many people with ADD unconsciously play "ADD games." These strategies are designed to create conflict to boost adrenaline and stimulate the frontal lobes. He has names for these games such as "I bet I can get you to yell at me or hit me"; "You can't make me do it"; and "Fighting as foreplay."

Another non-sensory arousal strategy that often goes unrecognized is our own thinking. The arousal from emotions generated from our own thoughts can be highly stimulating and motivating. Fear, joy, jealousy, anger, anxiety, indignation, hope, and curiosity are all powerful emotions that save us from boredom. They can be in response to what's happening around us, or we can generate them at any time while anticipating a problem or ruminating on an old one.

One of the reasons our own thoughts are such an effective source of arousal is because of all the strategies, they are the most immediately available. For instance, they can lead to the pleasure experienced from a daydream in the middle of the workday. Like the jungle gym during recess, a daydream offers a rejuvenating respite from the tedium of a particular task. On the other hand, our thoughts can also lead to problems and stress. We may obsess on problems, real or imagined, and make our lives miserable. Whether our thoughts lead us to pleasure or pain, either way they save us from boredom.

Fidget to Focus

Fidgeting is the natural rhythm of life. Dr. Edward Hallowell, co-author with Dr. John Ratey of *Delivered from Distraction* and other books on ADD, describes the ADD life as having a surplus of attention that is often unfocused. At other times, this attention can be extraordinarily hyperfocused. Unfortunately, despite this abundant ability to attend to things, the majority of activities that get started remain unfinished.

In the book, Hallowell describes life with ADD this way:

...You're spilling over all the time. You're drumming your fingers, tapping your feet, humming a song, whistling, looking here, looking there, scratching, stretching, doodling, and people think you're not interested, but all you're doing is spilling over so that you can pay attention. I can pay a lot better attention when I'm taking a walk or listening to music or even when I'm in a crowded, noisy room than when I'm still and surrounded by silence. God save me from the reading rooms....The only thing that saves it is that so many of the people who use (them) have ADD that there's a constant soothing bustle.

When we fidget in order to focus, the fidgeting results in the short-term modulation of our disregulated neurological system. This is, at least, what we think is going on knowing what we do about neurology. As we talked about in earlier chapters, the disregulation happens when there is not enough stimulation for the feedback loops in our brains to sustain adequate biochemical activity. When we are underaroused, the sense we are predominantly using is operating ineffectively in that moment. For instance, if our minds are not able to sustain focus during a lecture, this happens because our auditory processing is failing to keep us sufficiently stimulated, despite the level of importance of the event. In simpler terms, the activity may be interesting, just not interesting enough to keep our attention.

Respectful, Effective Fidgeting

An effective fidget needs to be both respectful of others and functional. It needs to be both situationally appropriate and effective. By applying a simultaneous sensory-motor stimulation strategy, easy to remember as the four S's, the goals is first, to not interrupt others, and second, to create a stimulating event that arouses and activates the brain, thus creating the ability to sustain interest where before we could not. In simplest terms, an effective fidget is a second sensory-motor activity we engage in to support the first. So which of the senses do we use? How do we choose an effective fidget?

Let's imagine a college student who is struggling to pay attention during a lecture. If he were to choose putting on his headphones and listening to his favorite CD as his strategy, it would likely fail. It would fail because the strategy would be competing for, not supporting, the sensory activity or modality required for the primary activity. He would no longer be able to listen to the lecture because he would be listening to his music.

However, if he pulled out his PDA and started playing a game, would this match what he needed? Yes, possibly. It would depend upon whether the game became his primary interest. For instance, if he began to focus on winning the game, then he would most likely win the game but lose the lecture. If, however, he were able to play the game discreetly with no investment in the outcome, the visual-motor function would temporarily stimulate brain activity to allow for greater focus.

An even better strategy would be to doodle on his notes while he listened. By using either of these visual-motor fidgets, he would likely be able to stay focused and remember a larger majority of the lecture material.

Fidget to Focus Strategies

Since the story of playing Nintendo first sparked our curiosity, we have shared it with whoever would listen. This has led, over the years, to many conversations about similar problems and strategies. From years of discussions and storytelling with members of ADD support groups, with family, and with friends, these are just some of the strategies reported to be helpful in successfully negotiating the dull, the tedious, and the mundane.

Movement Strategies

The most powerful of sensory strategies involve movement and engage our vestibular and proprioceptive senses. These rhythmic, repetitive actions range from large motor movements, as when we walk or run, to the very fine and almost imperceptible motor movements that occur as we continually adjust to keep ourselves balanced and upright.

A movement strategy commonly seen in classrooms, meeting rooms, and lecture halls around the world is the fidgety leg. When we take this strategy of rhythmic leg movement and expand it into full-on walking, many of us will notice that it helps improve our ability to concentrate for extended periods in conversation. This strategy was famously employed by Aristotle who conducted discussions while walking about the Lyceum of ancient Athens. Some of us find it difficult to have extended phone conversations unless we are pacing back and forth. A CEO we know of prefers to discuss business with his customers while on long-distance bike rides. Needless to say, his customers are of like mind. Some parents have found that the simple act of standing rather than sitting allows their child to remain happily at the dinner table.

Some long-distance runners with ADD have reported an improved ability to focus for over an hour following their run. One very restless professional football player once said that by combining his training as a defensive back with his ADD ability to see everything and move at the same time, he could be highly successful for the time it takes to run one play—about twenty seconds. Many of us have found that activities like yoga, aikido, and Tai Chi have been very helpful for increasing concentration and relaxation.

The more subtle aspects of movement involve challenging gravity. They are in play when we find improved focus while standing or while sitting erect in our chairs rather than reclining in them. This strategy of challenging gravity is most apparent when someone is balancing on the two back legs of a chair. Rather than restricting this activity, we encourage finding an unbreakable chair to use for this purpose, and seeing if attention and focus improve. Some therapists recommend using a large rubber exercise ball instead of a chair to sit on while doing deskwork. A more discreet, cushion-like version called a "Disc 'O' Sit" can be used to similar effect.

Some adults with ADD have reported using a gravity-challenging strategy to help them fall asleep. When lying on their side, they simply raise one arm straight in the air as if they were waiting to be called on by a teacher. This arm is then balanced in this state with very slight muscular movements. Holding this position requires just minor attention, just enough to distract from thoughts of the day, and those slight muscular movements are just mild enough stimulation that they find they can relax and fall asleep.

Movement strategies also encompasses fine motor movements that are sometimes obvious and sometimes not. Few of us may notice someone who is doodling while taking notes. However, we *are* likely to notice, and be irritated by, the person who is tapping or clicking their pen repeatedly. Finding a fidget strategy that works in the moment without distracting others can be a challenge.

Rita reported that when she knitted under the table during long, boring meetings at the office, she was able to listen better and remember more of the meeting. She also noticed that if she started to care how the knitting looked, she stopped paying attention to what was going on in the meeting. Since her priority was her work, her goal then became to simply maintain a discreet and constant movement of her hands while she listened to her boss talk.

During an initial assessment interview for ADD, Joe mentioned how his restlessness and drumming fingers nearly cost him his marriage. (Not surprisingly, it has been suggested that there exists a high incidence of ADD among professional drummers!) After an hour interview, the therapist indicated to Joe that he had not fidgeted once during the interview. Joe smiled broadly and tapping the end of his boot said, "Steel-toed boots. You can't see them, but my toes are wiggling constantly!" This solution had offered him an alternative to his restless finger drumming and tapping, and helped save his marriage.

Another region of the body where we see a high level of rhythmic repetitive movement is in the mouth. Adults smoke or sip drinks. Children suck on just about anything. Biting or chewing on fingernails, lips, inside of cheeks, pens, pencils, paper, and gum are also common strategies.

A recently published study by two groups of British researchers found that chewing gum improved critical thinking and working memory, both frontal lobe functions. They concluded that the act of chewing gum increased heart rate and improved the delivery of oxygen and glucose to the brain. Occupational therapists working with children have known for years the potential focusing benefits of chewing gum while reading or test taking.

Gerald was a highly trained physician. His specialty was in microsurgery, but he rarely was able to operate because he could not stand still for the time it would take to do the surgeries. Frustrated as a surgeon, he found instead that he was very successful as an emergency room doctor. He was great in a crisis situation when a desperately sick or injured patient would come in the door, but he needed a great deal of support and assistance from the nurses during the lulls. One day the nurses discovered that his focus improved when he chewed gum. So, at the beginning of each shift, they began offering it to him without telling him why. After researching these baffling behaviors, they realized he might have ADD. They shared their concerns and observations with him, and recommended he get an evaluation. He did get the evaluation and, with a new understanding of himself, new strategies, and medication, Gerald was able to successfully return to performing microsurgery.

Sight Strategies

Years ago, when an otherwise rambunctious child could sit still for hours while watching television, it was thought he or she could not possibly have this disorder. We have since learned that the ability to watch television quietly is not inconsistent with having ADD. We now understand that watching an interesting, visually stimulating television show provides the necessary sensory activation that allows us to sit still and attend. Under these circumstances, there is no need for additional motor movement to facilitate focus and decrease restlessness.

Other sight strategies involve momentary noticing of events in the environment. For instance, we might repeatedly glance out the window during class, or over our dinner partner's shoulder in a restaurant, or we might notice all sorts of things along the side of the road while driving. We might turn a television on in the background with no intension of actually watching it. The television is not the primary focus of our attention, but supplies visual and perhaps auditory stimulation.

Professional organizers trained in helping students and adults with ADD recognize the importance of visual cues to direct, differentiate, and focus attention on essential elements in their environment. The organizer may suggest photos of contents on storage boxes or, even better, see-through containers. They may rearrange closets so everything is in view, not hidden in drawers and boxes. They may also suggest a variety of colorful markers to use in the client's date book that will help the client notice and remember important appointments. Post-its placed in strategic places are another visual strategy that many of us with ADD use successfully. We've even heard of people who keep dry-erase markers and use them on the bathroom mirror because that's the place they successfully notice reminders!

Sound Strategies

How many parents have heard this familiar refrain: "But Mom, I can concentrate better on my homework if I'm listening to music!" To those without ADD this may make no sense, but those of us with ADD know it's true. Imagine reading a boring history textbook. For those of us with ADD, most likely after a few sentences our minds begin to wander. What if, rather than drifting off into our own thoughts, we noticed the music in the background? The attraction is apparent because this music is pleasurable, familiar, and, most importantly, ours. The beat is distinct and, if there are words, we already know them. The recognition of the familiar music soon becomes less than interesting and our thoughts return to the reading. All of this happens within moments and is repeated frequently while reading. This auditory rhythm allows for sustained attention while reading.

Whistling, humming, singing, and talking are effective ways to stay on task during boring activities. In school, we learn to read by first identifying sounds, then words, which eventually come together as sentences. Over time, the expectation is to read silently while hearing the words in our head. When reading, one way to improve focus is to read out loud. The impact of seeing, hearing, and saying the words is a multisensory strategy that can make a huge difference. Some of us find that even reading aloud isn't enough. Rather than droning on and on, we must add drama and pacing to the words in order to make it interesting.

Perhaps one of the most dramatic and effective uses of background noise came from Ted, who worked for a mobile detailing outfit, going to client's homes or businesses and washing their cars. He made a reasonable living at it, but washing and waxing cars was boring work, and he often found himself just standing there, daydreaming. He began to wonder how much income he lost every day, drifting off like that. After hearing other stories about *Fidget to Focus*, he bought a portable cassette player with headphones. He also bought a tape of white noise, a sort of whooshing rhythmic noise that he liked. He put the sound down low, so it remained in the background, and began monitoring his time on the job. After one month, he found his income had increased by 25 percent! Ted eventually graduated to other forms of background sound, but, after discovering how well this worked, never gave up using auditory strategies for staying focused on the job.

Touch Strategies

While touch strategies are often connected with movement, there is a distinct tactile, textural, or even temperature aspect to effective touch strategies. The student who plays with his or her hair during class may be using the rhythmic twirling as a touch strategy. The repeated little vibration of clicking a retractable pen again and again is a touch strategy, coupled with movement and sound. Fiddling with our jewelry or watches or touching our faces are touch strategies we use all the time. Pets or stuffed toys are often selected for touch strategies because of their texture. Some of us find we can write easily and for a long time with one kind of writing implement, due to the fit in the hand and the feel of the tip gliding over the paper, but not with another. Some of us prefer keyboards.

Temperature is another strategy we use without thinking about it. Whether it is splashing cold water on our faces to wake ourselves up, or a hot shower in the morning to get ourselves going, water and water temperature work for many of us. How many of us feel more alert after opening a window and getting a blast of cool fresh air in our faces and sinuses? Or when we find ourselves too warm and drifty, how many of us shed our sweater or jacket in order to cool down and be able to concentrate again?

One day care provider we know carefully and firmly sewed little fidgets to one corner of each blanket she provided her charges at nap time. On one was a piece of satin. On another, an appliquéd woolly lamb. On a third was a cute button. Each child had a favorite blanket, and would drift off to sleep with that corner of the blanket between his or her fingers.

Jim told us that he likes to absently rub a wrinkle of his trousers between his thumb and middle finger while he talks. His favorite trousers are made of twill. On learning about *Fidget to Focus*, he realized this was because the little ridges in the twill cause a very small, pleasant vibration as he rubs it back and forth between his fingers, which helps him stay present and in the conversation.

George is an attorney who mostly does litigation for his firm. Having ADD, he enjoys this work as it is highly stimulating and interesting. Sometimes, however, the demand for thoughtful deliberation requires an extra effort. Fearing he would lose track of what he was saying in these moments, he fell upon the following strategy. He calls it his "silkies." George loves the feel of silk and buys shirts that have at least some silk in them. As he speaks, he takes the cuff of one of his sleeves with his thumb and forefinger and gently rubs the cloth. This action increases his concentration while not distracting from his presentation, because it appears as if he is simply adjusting his shirt cuff.

Taste Strategies

Many of us use a variety of taste strategies without even realizing it. We sip on our favorite drink, be it water, tea, coffee, or soda (decaffeinated or otherwise). We indulge in our favorite snack or treat, be it crunchy or chewy, salty, sour, or sweet. These are the common strategies many of us use to keep us going through the day.

Some of us have noticed that the more intense flavors are particularly alerting. These strategies tend to be striking when they are first used. For instance, the intense flavor of Altoids or sour lemon drops may be used during a meeting when we are concerned we might become drowsy. Many of us keep such treats in our desk or purse for just such occasions.

On learning about *Fidget to Focus*, Kathleen briefly looked surprised, letting out a stunned, "oh my &%*!" as a certain memory rushed back to her. Then she shared her memories of her third-grade teacher. Before each test, the teacher would hand out sour lemon drops. Other children simply liked the treat, but Kathleen remembers the tart flavor helping her to concentrate. She always did well on those tests, and remembered that teacher and class fondly.

Smell Strategies

As smell is the most primitive of the senses, our response can be very visceral, immediate, and powerful. Fresh air can clear the head. We have aromatic salves to clear the sinuses. There is nothing like the pungent smell of ammonia used in smelling salts to arouse someone after passing out. Aromatherapy is used to both stimulate and calm us. Lemon oil is used to alert us if we are feeling sluggish, and lavender oil is used to encourage relaxation.

Smell strategies are all around us, although we are typically not terribly aware of them. Our modern society is full of ways to eliminate unwanted odors and add pleasing ones: room fresheners, scented candles, potpourris, perfumes, and colognes. These are popular because of their positive effect on us.

Although we don't have many stories of people using smell specifically as a fidget strategy, we do have one. A youngster attributed being able to spend more time on her homework due to her markers that smelled like fruit: blue smelled like blueberry, red like cherry, black like licorice, etc. As she lifted the marker to smell it better, she would leave behind first a blue dot, then a red one, then a black one. Her mother could always tell when she'd been working hard because of the multicolored smear on the end of her nose!

Time Strategies

Perhaps one of the most intriguing and challenging of all the strategies is our sense of time. Problems with estimating and sensing time passing are a hallmark of ADD. Yet, timing is everything. A sense of time enables us to wait more successfully. The ability to wait enables us to inhibit our immediate reactions more successfully. A sense of time allows us a past and a future. It creates space in which to plan our actions, and space in which to anticipate consequences of our actions. It comes into play when we arrive on time for a surprise birthday party, finish a paper by the due date, decide to not chase a ball into the street, or anticipate the rhythm in the music we play.

We all know the parable of "The Tortoise and the Hare," of how an energetic hare challenges a sedate tortoise to a footrace and how the hare, after sprinting off and getting well down the road, decides to take a nap. And we all know how he wakes up later on only to find the tortoise has won the race while he slept. The tortoise is the hero of this story. Slow and steady, we are taught, wins the race. The problem is, there are more ways to be in this world than simply slow and steady.

One day at school, Jason broke into tears crying, "I will never be the tortoise!" Jason had just heard this parable for the first time and, after telling the story, Jason's teacher predictably went on to explain that this story teaches a very important lesson: slow and steady wins the race. Jason explained through his tears that he would never be slow or steady. In fact, as he listened to the story, he was hoping the hare would win because the rabbit reminded him of himself.

Jason frequently would get excited at the beginning of projects, but very distracted in the middle and have a hard time finishing them. Like the hare, Jason would also estimate time poorly, often discovering this much too late. Jason could be focused when he was really excited and motivated to do something. But when he was not, Jason felt just like the hare, running and napping and seeming never to cross the finish line. Rather than slow and steady, swift and playful would be better descriptors of Jason and the hare.

Jason, with great wisdom, decided not to try to change his innate timing or rhythm. Rather than trying to be slow and steady, Jason decided to find ways to be a better hare. He learned that to win the race, he had to develop and be aware of his own internal rhythms. He learned to avoid both the boredom of a slow and steady pace and the panic of procrastination. More importantly, he learned simply to never run a long-distance race. Jason found that breaking a large race down into a series of small races worked well for him. By sprinting against the clock while engaged in some activity, then resting or doing something else, Jason found he could maintain his interest, avoid the boredom, and achieve his goals.

By racing time we can effectively move from tedium to attention. Try it yourself. When next you sit down to clear out your e-mail inbox, rather than setting out to read all of the e-mails, not stopping until you are done, allow yourself ten minutes to clear out just the junk mail. Set a timer and race the clock. The race adds excitement. Be sure to do what you promised yourself, and end when the timer goes off. Reward yourself with moving on to another task or taking a brief break. Later you can go back and do it again with a different category of e-mail.

The practice of estimating how long it takes to complete tasks is also a benefit of "sprinting." With a clear goal and a clear time frame, we cultivate in ourselves a better ability to estimate how long our daily tasks take. In addition to getting more done, this practice in time sense will pay off in letting us be on time more of the time.

By creating sprints in our lives, we can effectively transform any tedious task into a challenging one, making it interesting and therefore do-able for those of us with ADD. We don't have to be tortoises to win the race; we just have to be smarter hares.

Companion Strategies

The ultimate fidget, many people find, is the company of another person. The company of someone who is doing a similar task with us or alongside us can be the best and sometimes only way to keep us alert and on task. In addition, the presence of the other person creates a sense of accountability that many of us find helpful.

If we have trouble getting ourselves into a physical fitness regimen, a well-known strategy is to get an exercise partner. Studying with a study-buddy in the library or a coffee shop is just the ticket for some. Sharing chores makes them interesting enough that the laundry may well get washed, dried, *and* put away. A lively phone conversation can keep us going when we have tedious housework to do, or can be used as a pick-me-up after an hour of desk work.

Or, if we have ADD and want to write a book, collaborating may be the one way to keep it interesting enough long enough that we actually follow through!

Review

* Sensory strategies to improve health, well-being, and state of mind date back to earliest civilizations.

* From the color we choose for fire trucks or hospital rooms, to the scents we choose to wear or fill our homes with, to Muzak and iPods, sensory stimulation strategies are already an integral part of our lives.

* Some of the strategies we use to stimulate ourselves into interest and thus action, e.g. procrastination or emotional conflict, can have undesirable side effects. Other stimulation strategies with undesirable side effects include nicotine, street drugs, and behavioral addictions such as computers, eating, shopping, gambling, and sex.

* Movement is one of our most effective strategies. Many people have noticed how standing, walking, or running can make a huge difference in their ability to attend, even after the activity has stopped. Recess can be the most effective way to help a child sit still and attend for the rest of the day.

* Effective fidgeting uses a second sensory-motor activity, one other than that needed for our primary activity, to help us stay alert and focused on that primary activity. These secondary activities might include listening to our favorite music while we do homework or housework, doodling in our notebooks while we listen to a lecture, or chewing gum while we take a test.

* Respectful fidgeting needs to be situationally appropriate and should not bother or distract those around us.

CHAPTER 7

Strategies for Living with ADD

Learning to Fidget

In the last chapter, we took a look at the strategies we use for self-regulation, the strategies we use to place ourselves in an optimal state for our current activity. We looked at traditional, modern, and non-sensory strategies. Most importantly, for the purposes of this book, we learned about sensory-motor strategies. In this chapter, we will talk about how to translate specific sensory-motor strategies into effective strategies for everyday life.

Sensory-motor strategies, the ones we call "fidgets," are the most natural and ubiquitous self-regulating strategies of all. Therefore, the first step in learning to use these strategies effectively is to give ourselves *permission* to fidget. Not only that, but we must give ourselves permission to fidget without fear or shame. We must send packing those voices that scold "Sit still!" and "Look at me when I'm talking to you!" and "Don't try to do two things at once!" We must recognize that these simultaneous sensory-motor activities are a perfectly natural adjustment in those times when the current activity is underwhelming, when it is just not interesting enough to sustain our attention.

Second, we must find our own unique, natural, sensory-motor rhythms and strategies. When we become aware of our fidgeting through this lens, we begin to notice which simultaneous activity works. We also begin to identify when it works, and the situation in which it works best. For example, if we find listening to a presentation tedious, our sense of hearing alone is failing to keep us alert. When this happens, is our simultaneous activity more likely to be noticing what other people are doing, wiggling a foot, or fiddling with coins in our pocket?

We need to remember that what works for someone else may not work for us, and therefore we must find our own strategies. We can identify these by recognizing which is our strongest or most alerting sense, and which is our least. When we are forced to use our least alerting sense, a simultaneous strategy that uses our most alerting sense will be the most effective.

Next, we must educate those around us about *Fidget to Focus*. For many people, the idea that a simultaneous sensory-motor activity will help our ability to focus will be counterintuitive. After all, it's common sense that we can concentrate better if we just do one thing at a time. Get rid of those distractions! It's true that many people are successful only when they do one thing at a time, but for us the opposite is usually true. We can't make ourselves into tortoises, and others can't make themselves into hares. We need to respect the fact that there is neural diversity, that different people have different ways of doing things, not just from preference or contrariness, but from need.

Finally, managing ADD involves recognizing that we have choices and taking action. Without making proactive choices, the strategies we use in challenging moments are chosen by default, by habit, or by whatever is most interesting at that moment. These strategies, when thoughtlessly chosen, can save us from boredom but can have undesirable consequences ranging from the lost time of daydreams to the devastations of addictions. How much more effective and powerful it is to understand what is going on in our brains and to proactively choose an appropriate strategy. How much more constructive and happier the outcome!

To illustrate what we are talking about, enrich understanding, and spark imaginations, we have compiled stories collected from many years of sharing these ideas with patients, clients, friends, and family. These are stories of the simultaneous sensory-motor stimulation strategies people have found to be effective in their own lives. Here we have organized them by setting, with situations that are often problematic for people with ADD: home, falling asleep, waking up, school, work, and relationships.

Fidget Strategies at Home

Wilma says she cleans her house the ADD way. Each Saturday, she begins promptly at 9 a.m. and ends at noon. During this time, her husband takes the children to their sporting events or to the park. At noon, Wilma's best friend comes to pick her up for lunch. This is their special time for getting together. The lunch also carries a special significance because they agreed early on to not have lunch if she did not finish her housecleaning. Wilma remembers the day this happened. Somehow she was just not done when her friend came for her. Being her best friend, the other woman lived up to their agreement and left, but it was embarrassing to let her friend down and cause them to miss their special time together, and very disappointing. Wilma, like so many of us with ADD, felt ashamed. She decided right then that she would not let this ever happen again.

Wilma places a list of chores to be completed on her refrigerator. At 9 a.m., she turns up the music so she can hear it throughout the house and begins anywhere. She may start with washing dishes and, halfway through the process, realize that she needs a dish towel. When she goes to the laundry room to get a dish towel, she decides to start a load of laundry and notices that the floor of the laundry room needs to be swept. It's not important that Wilma finish the dishes first; her only concern is that when she finishes a chore, she marks it off on her list. Wilma realizes that she barely has enough time to clean the house in three hours. Given this built-in intensity combined with music in the background, she finds it to be a perfect *Fidget to Focus* house-cleaning strategy.

Sally deliberately does housework inefficiently because it just feels good to move, to climb the stairs many times, and to walk from one end of the house to another. She works from her home office, so she saves the dishes to do until mid-morning, when she needs some physical activity to re-energize her. Her friends have learned that when they go for lunch or coffee with her, after about an hour of sitting and enjoying the food, company, and conversation, it will be time to go for a walk. Otherwise, it will be hard for Sally to continue to enjoy herself.

Dorothy, and three women she knew from an online chat room, frustrated with their disorganization and undone household chores, came up with a novel idea. They decided to get together online for an hour each day. The first fifteen minutes were to discuss what they were going to complete around the home in the next half hour. Then they would get up and do what they said they were going to do. Finally, they would return to their computers for the last fifteen minutes to share and celebrate their successes. By building accountability and aware-ness of time into their strategy, these women were able to be successful at maintaining their focus and achieving their goals.

Clutter is often an issue in an ADD home. By clutter, we mean things that are left out to be dealt with, yet they never get attended to. The items that pile up often represent hope or possibilities. What is now clutter may once have been the start of an exciting project, or an item left out for a task to be done tomorrow, or junk mail that was saved because it informs about something we think we might do in the future. That pile on the kitchen counter, or the desk, or the dining table is thus an unmade decision that has taken physical form. It not only repre-sents clutter in our space, but also clutter in our time when we continue to spend mental resources thinking about those old hopes and possibilities. Clutter is, of course, a visual fidget, but it is one that drags us down rather than moves us forward. Clearing the clutter in our homes decreases the likelihood of having visual attractions/distractions that interrupt our current goals and objectives. By clearing out and simplifying our space and time, we are more available to focus on the present and the projects at hand.

Falling Asleep

Those of us with ADD know that falling asleep can be very difficult. Sleep difficulties are, in fact, a hallmark of ADD. We wish we could just lay our head down on the pillow and gently fall asleep, but for many of us it just doesn't happen that way. With our new understanding of ADD, however, this makes per-fect sense. Lying quietly in bed can result in an underactive brain state, which our brains unconsciously strive to stimulate. Some of us find our thoughts looping endlessly through the day's events or dwelling on concerns about tomorrow. Others experience it more physically, and just can't get comfortable enough to drift off. Others experience it as literally being too bored to fall asleep.

Fidget strategies work for falling asleep, just the way they work during the day, the goal being to help us achieve optimal arousal for a given activity. One mother reports that her daughter, who occasionally declared herself to be too bored to sleep, experimented with different sleeping venues: the floor, the couch, and once even the bathtub. Changing where she slept created just enough novelty that the strategy worked every time.

Bill uses the television to fall asleep. He likes the laugh track from Jay Leno's monologue the best, finding David Letterman too loud and too rowdy. Marcia uses the television as well, but she doesn't watch it or listen to it. It's simply the flicker of the light in the background that helps her fall asleep. Ed generally watches a mystery or science-fiction show that has plenty of action. He's noticed that to be effective for him, the show needs to be interesting, but not too interesting. Then the visual activity becomes both mildly entertaining and relaxing. The result is he falls asleep. Others report using the radio or the sound of a fan to fall asleep.

Thom Hartmann writes in his *Complete Guide to ADD* that he long ago discovered he could fall asleep most easily if he read something truly boring. For years he has subscribed to *Scientific American Magazine*, finding it much cheaper than sleeping pills. We wonder if he is actually using Ed's strategy of needing his reading to be interesting, but not too interesting. One of us has relied on this strategy herself, falling asleep for years while reading *Science News*.

Joan has always been an advocate of meditation. She found, however, that the repetitive mantras she used so successfully during the day to relax were ineffective for helping her fall asleep. When she switched meditation techniques and began using guided imagery instead, she found it easy to fall asleep. Joan suggests that the imagery one uses be unpredictable. For her, it begins as a hike up a mountain trail while noticing the white clouds against the blue sky, the scent of pine trees as they sway in the breeze, the crunch of pine needles underfoot, and the sound of a gray squirrel scolding her intrusion into his forest. Besides the heightened level of sensory awareness, the trail is different every night. The stimulation that comes from the unexpected and imagined events often puts her asleep long before she "finishes" the hike.

Still others, like Gary, prefer to use gentle, repetitive movement to fall asleep. Gary finds that rubbing the silken edge of his blanket or simply wiggling his toes works well for him. Then there is the strategy we mentioned in the previous chapter of raising an arm straight toward the ceiling as if waiting to be called on by a teacher. The very slight muscular movements required to hold the arm balanced in that position create a mildly interesting yet relaxing activity, exactly the kind of fidget that can make falling asleep easier.

Waking Up

In perfect and cruel symmetry, just as falling asleep can be a problem, awakening can be a major bugaboo with ADD.

A common strategy for those of us on meds is to set two alarms, one for taking meds that have been set out on the bedside table the night before and one for actually getting up. But sometimes not even this strategy works. What do we do if this is our problem and we don't have a spouse or parent to roust us at the appropriate time?

A novel strategy to deal with this particular problem was proposed in an adult ADD support group. As they discussed this issue, it was quickly acknowledged that simply using an alarm clock was laughable. Then people wondered if this clock could be placed just out of reach of the bed so it would be impossible to just reach out and hit the snooze button. Then it was suggested that another alarm clock be strategically placed across the room to ring just seconds after the first one was turned off.

However, for this group not even the out-of-reach two-alarm system seemed reliable enough. The group decided that still another alarm clock should be placed in the bathroom and synchronized so that it would ring just seconds after the second clock. This would ensure the person would make it all the way to the bathroom without getting back into bed. This Rube Goldberg sequence was finally determined to be the best strategy.

As the group was realizing this plan was probably not one that anyone would actually implement, a young man in the back of the room said, "I know what works." He went on to explain that before he went to bed, he drank two large glasses of water. The room was shocked with disbelief, then burst into gales of laughter. When the laughter died out, he cheerfully challenged the others to try it. The next month, 80 percent of those who tried the "take two glasses of water at bedtime" strategy found they had no trouble at all getting up in the morning. Unlike the buzz of an alarm clock, there was no denying the call of nature!

Some of us just don't respond to sounds when we are asleep. Nothing we try works. Martha could never rouse to an alarm. She knew that being touched was her most reliable way of awakening, but she lived alone. She finally discovered the technology that is nominally intended for the Deaf community. She now uses a vibrating alarm that goes off under her pillow when it's time to wake up. Her particular alarm system also has a tabletop unit with a very loud and variable alarm sound and a flashing light. With all three, she can now reliably arise on time for the first time in her adult life.

Fidget Strategies at School

For many young students, simply sitting and listening constitutes one of the most difficult tasks they encounter. Learning is by nature a multisensory event. The more we engage the senses, the greater the likelihood of retaining the material. Dottie Walters, doyenne of highly paid public speakers, advises that an audience will retain 20 percent of what it hears, 30 percent of what it sees, 50 percent of what it hears and sees, and 80 percent of what it hears and sees and does. These numbers are for adult audiences, whose sensory-motor needs are significantly less than those of children.

Many teachers do employ multisensory teaching strategies in their classrooms. For example, strategies for increasing focus while reading may include incorporating music in the background, sitting on an exercise ball and moving gently, chewing gum, squeezing a fidget ball, standing and swaying, or reading aloud with enthusiasm. In one grade school we know of, the teachers keep baskets of fidget toys in their rooms. Students are allowed to have one fidget toy with them at their desk during class, and return it on their way out. A prep school we know of, recognizing that many students can study better while listening to music, now allows the use of iPods or similar personal music devices while studying in the library, with a strict caveat that if they are not used respectfully, they will be confiscated!

For students, transitions between activities can represent the most difficult times in a school day. Some of the most challenging occur when going from a high arousal event to a low arousal event, such as transitioning from recess back into the classroom. The first step here is to teach students to anticipate these problems. By anticipating these events, these ADD students can begin to develop a set of activating strategies to assist them.

Some teachers will do a transition for the whole class. Once inside and at their desks, the teacher will lead all the children through some stretching exercises or other activity before sitting and writing. Some of the subtler strategies that we know have worked for some students include a pre-assigned task like handing out or collecting papers from each desk. While other students are getting settled at their desks, this might be a time when an ADD child would carry a note to the main office. One teacher reported simply having a list taped to the top of each desk that described the standard steps to be prepared for the next subject. The real trick was that she laminated all of these lists before taping them to the desks so that the students could mark them as they completed each step. The marks later were erased to be ready for the next transition.

One fourth-grade student named Dave found that his best strategy was quite simple. Without others knowing it, he would race to be the first one ready after the transition. His teacher would give him points for being first, second, or third.

For young students, it is essential for neurological development that they get the exercise and movement that comes from daily recess. It is important to be active and to join with others in playing games or a sport. Dr. John Ratey, author of *A User's Guide to the Brain*, says if you won't exercise for your body, exercise for your brain. Not only do aerobic exercise and hard muscular work make a difference, but nutritious breakfasts, snacks, and lunches can also have a major impact on a child's ability to focus in the classroom.

As students get older, the demands for sequencing, planning, and timing are greater. Organizing a workbook, term paper, or large project can be one of the most difficult tasks asked of these students. Without the assistance of caring parents and friends, projects can easily be put off until the last minute. Procrastination becomes the default strategy. And it often works. Many ADD students report some success by using the natural neural stimulation of adrenaline that comes from waiting until the last few hours to complete the project.

By understanding why procrastination works, we are more capable of applying fidget strategies in our own time instead of waiting until the last minute. For example, rather than breaking a large project down into five parts, make it ten parts, but place a strict time limit on each part. By intensifying time, we increase our awareness of the sense of time. Being accountable to someone else is another way of increasing our focus on the task, much as if we were in a race.

As a college student with ADD, Rich struggled to stay caught up in school. He often didn't complete all the reading assignments, and his homework was sometimes incomplete or not turned in. Rich knew that he would have to make a change, or change his life dream of continuing on to graduate school. He remembered he had been very successful in his structured nine-to-five summer job, so Rich decided to make school more like that job. He started by creating a tight structure around his classroom schedule. While his friends went off for coffee after his early-morning class, Rich sat down to review the notes he had just taken and to prepare for his next class. Rather than studying late into the night, Rich would go to the library between classes to read and do homework. He discovered that reviewing the material immediately after the lecture made it easier to remember for the quiz at the end of the week. To vary his day, Rich would read standing up, walking around, or aloud in the park. He also found computer-based tools like voice-recognition technology and mind mapping software very helpful in expressing and organizing his thoughts.

Teaching ADD students to fidget effectively is to train them in two of the most important skills they can ever learn: self-monitoring and self-regulation. Once we understand about optimal alertness, we can begin training ourselves in self-monitoring. We can begin to notice when we're too bored or too overwhelmed. Once we understand about our brain's need for a certain level of stimulation, and how our natural sensory-motor activities can provide just the right amount for a given situation, we can begin to train ourselves in self-regulation, using resources that are always available to us. Part of learning to fidget effectively is learning to choose a fidget that not only works for us in that moment, but that is also situationally appropriate and respectful of those around us. In combining understanding of self-regulation with respectfulness to those around us, we also gain a much greater sense of self and self-respect.

Fidget Strategies at Work

Many people ask us what is the best job or the best career for someone with ADD. We recommend avoiding a job that involves data entry of repetitive numbers with no room for error. Most often the answer has relatively little to do with what the job is, and more to do with how you make your work match what you need.

Perhaps the best example of work ideally suited to someone with ADD would be the work that occurs in a hospital's emergency room. First, the environment has a cycle or rhythm of crisis to calm. Second, the physical environment is very structured. Everything has a place, so clutter is minimal. Third, the demand for planning and organizing around who comes in the door, or what happens once they leave, is of little concern in the emergency room. This allows for the intense focus to remain on what's immediately in front of the staff. Finally, for a person with ADD who pays attention to everything, crisis is comfortable. With the added stimulation from the intense environment, focus actually improves. The work is often done standing up and requires a skillful blend of knowledge, training, and thinking out-of-the-box. Triage is a medical term that involves many people multitasking to organize and manage patients' needs. This model of collaborative effort is a powerful part of the perfect ADD work environment. Any highly active and structured work environment, especially one with high accountability like firefighting, professional team sports, or even the military have proven to be good work situations and safe havens for people with ADD.

Sam was a salesman who was quite successful at his door-to-door efforts to sell insulation and a new paint job to homeowners. Unfortunately, with his ADD, Sam had great difficulty following through to complete the sales transactions. His boss called him in one day to give Sam the bad news that despite his great talent, he was going to be fired. The company just could not afford the reputation of failed promises in combination with lost transactions. In the meantime, Sam had sought help for his ADD and learned the importance of focusing on his talents. Before his boss could speak, Sam offered to take a demotion to do phone sales. This meant that he would be primarily responsible for the initial contact while handing off the follow-up to another salesman. While this action lowered his income dramatically, it placed Sam in the heart of what he did the best. Sam loved to talk. Within three months, Sam's income had doubled. Without the strain of the tedious sales follow-up, he could now focus entirely on connecting with people. He loved them, and they loved him!

Fidget Strategies in Relationships

The art of maintaining a relationship when ADD is present is hard for many of us, yet it is also simple. Every day we must make a choice to be interesting and interested. When we work to be curious, playful, and thoughtful, we maintain the highest level of regard for our partner and for ourselves. The first step in this process is to begin creating a flexible structure that blends passion with varying interests and responsibilities.

Jim and Alyssa were planning their honeymoon. As a part of their premarital counseling assignment, they worked separately to identify their most exciting and romantic ideas for the honeymoon. Hawaii was on the top of both their lists. Their counselor congratulated them on their similar interest in location and asked Jim to continue sharing his ideal honeymoon.

With excitement, and a touch of ADD, Jim launched into a day that would begin before sunrise to get to the top of the volcano so they could mountain bike down the mountain as the sun rose. After a brief breakfast, they would take the Jeep and run some back trails to a spot only locals know that would offer the best snorkeling and surfing. They would find lunch on their way back and, after a brief rest, hike three miles to a very special waterfall. Jim figured they would be back just in time to catch the luau at the nearby resort.

Before he could even begin to share the events he had planned for their second day, he caught a glimpse of Alyssa's face. She was shocked and overwhelmed. Her idea of a perfect honeymoon began with a leisurely morning with breakfast in bed. The day would begin about eleven in the morning with a quick dip in the pool and a relaxing sauna. This would be followed by finding the perfect book in the gift shop and reading for several hours by the pool or at the beach. After soaking up the sun, a refreshing swim and a massage would cap off the afternoon. Before she could say more about the evening, Jim stopped her. He realized that he could not possibly sit through her honeymoon. Alyssa knew she could not keep up with his.

Finding the balance in relationships is not always easy when ADD is involved. What Jim needs to stay interested is very different than what Alyssa needs. In finding the balance, it is first necessary to identify the rhythms in the relationship. Jim needs a greater level of activity and excitement than Alyssa. Alyssa has a clear sense of her needs for the calm and soothing. While their ideas of the perfect honeymoon may appear to be miles apart, their extreme differences can actually create a fine sense of balance in their relationship. It is important to honor the differences.

Alyssa and Jim accepted the challenge of blending the two honeymoons; they decided not to compromise by finding some middle ground where both would be moderately satisfied. In fact, they each decided to taste the other's honeymoon, a stretch that was challenging for both of them. It began with an early-morning bike ride, followed by a sauna and massage. Jim agreed to buy a science-fiction book to read occasionally and Alyssa agreed to get hiking boots. While at the beach, he would surf while she would read, and sometimes they would snorkel together. They found that by honoring their differences and trying each others dream honeymoon, they each were challenged and excited to discover more about each other as well as themselves.

Neal and Mary had been married for three years. Six months ago, she had their first child. They laid their unsigned divorce papers on the therapist's table and asked for help. Mary was fed up with Neal's broken promises. In tears, she explained that she would ask Neal to stop at the market on his way home to pick up basic supplies for meals and for the baby, but Neal would frequently forget. In an effort to get him to remember, she would call him frequently during his busy day. She was beginning to feel like a nag and she hated it. Neal began to resent her inter-rupting calls, unaware of how much Mary also resented making the calls. The final straw came when at breakfast she asked Neal to bring home some milk for the baby. Neal promised and then completely forgot. With all the complications of his busy day, Neal had no strategy for remembering the request from home.

Neal had recently been diagnosed with ADD and they had learned it was partly to blame for his poor organization and planning. His focus was intense while at work, which allowed him to be very successful. However, at home, or in the transition between work and home, Neal tended to be unfocused, which would set him up to forget to bring home the milk for his wife and baby. Mary held little hope for change.

In their therapy, they learned that being organized was only part of the picture. They also needed to create a method that would incorporate simple strategies that would make things interesting and challenging. Neal knew that his business was mostly conducted over the phone. He would first check his messages in the morning, then work to pick up every call throughout the day. If a message came in during lunch, his first task after lunch would be to return the call. Since this habit was already so well established, Mary thought perhaps they could take advantage of it. They developed a strategy that she would leave a message for anything she needed him to do on his way home on his machine. Neal's last task of the day would then be to listen to the message and return the message counter to zero. Neal would then write the message on a fluorescent Post-it note and place it in a clearly visible location in his car so he would not forget to bring home the milk or diapers or whatever Mary needed.

This strategy worked so well that they began telling humorous stories, like when Mary was standing next to Neal in the morning and she asked him to bring home the milk. Only this time, she would first pick up the phone, call the answering machine at his office, and then ask him to bring home the milk. As promises were kept, trust was regained and the divorce papers were burned.

The therapist knew his work was done when Neal shared an experience with Mary in their therapy session. He told her how he had become distracted at the end of the day. He hurried out of the office and forgotten to pick up the message from Mary about bringing home the milk. He arrived at home, pulled his car into the garage and realized he had not checked the messages. Realizing he was just about to break his promise, he called his message machine with his new cell phone, and checked for Mary's message. Then he backed out of the garage, without letting Mary know he had actually been that close to walking in the door empty handed, and went and ran the required errand. With a smile on his face, a spring in his step, and the milk in his arms, he arrived home a short while later. Neal was not going to tell Mary about the incident, but changed his mind when he realized this event really represented the passion and intensity of his commitment to Mary. As Mary and Neal got up to leave therapy for the last time, Mary pulled the therapist aside and whispered to him "I knew!"

Relationships are often at risk for becoming too familiar. While familiarity can be comforting, it can also be tedious and downright boring. When this happens, we turn to other things that attract our interest. Imagine trying to have a conversation over breakfast while one person has his or her attention on the crossword puzzle or finding a furniture ad. It can be extremely frustrating, not only the couple but to anyone within hearing distance. Under such circumstances, information can frequently be either miscommunicated or misunderstood or both.

Molly has ADD and knows that she does not tolerate boredom. Molly also knows she needs to get active and stimulated to
be able to focus in her conversations. Her husband, Ryan, would
often tell Molly how frustrated he felt in conversations with her
when she would look around, seemingly everywhere but at him.
To him, this meant she was not paying attention and clearly did
not care.

Another problem was that Ryan gets home late, so Molly felt
she rarely got a chance to talk to him. The solution was that
Molly and Ryan decided to get up and walk several miles
together before breakfast. Molly loved having more time to just
be with Ryan. She discovered that walking made it easier for her
to focus. She also found that when they walked and talked, Ryan
had less expectations of her to look at him. To the unobserving
eye, Ryan and Molly may simply look like a couple out for
exercise before breakfast. Molly and Ryan new it to be an ADD-
friendly way to allow them to enjoy each other more, and
perhaps even save their marriage.

Simple sensory-motor strategies can be very effective in
changing a relationship headed for the rocks into a focused and
happy partnership. But, as illustrated by the story of Jim and
Alyssa, finding the balance between the differing sensory needs
of each partner is not always easy when ADD is involved. In
finding the balance, it is necessary to identify and respect the
rhythms in the relationship and the differing needs for stimulation and activity of each partner. As we noted earlier, every day
we must make a choice to be interested and interesting. When
we work to be curious, playful, and thoughtful, we maintain the
highest level of regard for our partner and for ourselves. Building
a relationship based on this respect, and on mutual discovering of

common passions, brings interest to the conversations, discovery to vacations, and hope to all the tomorrows.

Structure, Brevity, Variety

Finally, in order to live most effectively with ADD, we should seek out or create environments and activities that complement and support our neurology. Create a life that has lots of room for movement, both physical and attentional. Enliven your environments with colors, views, and belongings that interest and please your eye. Be aware of sound environments and try to tailor them to your needs. If tastes or smells do it for you, keep a stock of favorites around. If you like finger fidgets, keep a variety handy in your desk, backpack, or purse, or choose clothing and jewelry that fill that need. For the tedious elements in life, use time sprint strategies to keep things interesting, and don't forget about the value of creating accountability. Seek to do this in all areas of your life, be it home, school, work, or in relationships.

In 1991 Clare Jones coined the phrase "structure, brevity, and variety" while recognizing the need for ADD students to have classroom environments that involve consistent structure, shorter lessons, and more interesting and varied material.

We now know that most people do not outgrow ADD. We also know that what works for students works for adults, but recognize that the lives of students and adults are different. To structure, brevity, and variety, we therefore add simplicity, passion, rhythm, and balance. As we grow older, life gets increasingly complicated, thereby necessitating the need for simplicity. Staying focused in complexity requires a balance between the rhythms or patterns of our lives and our passions.

Too much work would be deadly for those of us with ADD, but too much play is also destructive.

By seeking or creating good fidgeting environments, and by building these principles of structure, brevity, variety, simplicity, passion, rhythm, and balance into our lives, we can improve our focus, our behavior, our emotional equilibrium, and our ability to learn. As life becomes easier and we experience fewer derailments, we begin to feel less discouraged and demoralized. Fear and shame drop away; creativity soars. The greatest outcome of all may well be a sense of success and healthy self-esteem.

Review

* Fidgets are sensory-motor activities that help with self-regulation. They are the most natural and ubiquitous self-regulating strategies we have. They work for everyone, not just people with ADD.

* Because fidgets work, and work more healthfully than other alerting strategies that may be available to us, we must give ourselves permission to fidget.

* We are each wonderfully unique biological creatures. Not every strategy will work for every person, and no strategy will work for any one person all of the time. We therefore need to discover what works for each of us individually.

* We need to educate those around us about neural diversity and fidgeting to focus; that some of us, for neurological reasons, do better doing just one thing at a time, and others function better when doing two or more things at once.

* We have a responsibility to make choices for ourselves regarding how we will self-regulate, and to take effective action. This applies in all areas of our lives.

CHAPTER 8

Where Do We Go from Here?

The Rhythms of Life

When we talk about rhythms of life, what exactly do we mean? We mean that, like the changing of the seasons or the ebb and flow of the tides, which are never and always the same, we know the cycle will be repeated, not with the precise measured beat of a metronome, but with a certain predictability and reliability. We mean that like the intake and exhalation of our breath, like the repeated cycle of wakefulness and sleep, there are ubiquitous, cyclic patterns of activity in the simple, wonderful act of being human and alive.

Every day of our existence we experience rhythms of activity and rest, hunger and satiety, comfort and discomfort. When our biological systems are well-regulated, we adjust for changing circumstances with ease. For instance, our hearts speed up when we exercise, and then slow down again in rest. We experience hunger when our blood sugar drops, and then satiety when we have eaten. We experience a momentary startle at a loud sound in another room, and then relax as we recognize the sound of a door slamming. With ADD, however, some of our natural biochemical rhythms, specifically some of our natural neurochemical rhythms, are disregulated, which lead to the problems with attention, impulsiveness, and hyperactivity that we are all so familiar with.

ADD Fundamentally

Having ADD means that inattention, impulsivity, and hyperactivity are frequently our companions. We spend much of our time looking for ways to manage these often unwelcome visitors and the struggles they create in our lives. While many strategies work for a while, they never work for very long, and it often seems that just as we start to get ahead, something happens to trip us up. Life with ADD often feels like two steps forward and three steps back, which, because it happens again and again and again, is painful, discouraging, and demoralizing.

We now understand that ADD, far from being a "morbid defect of moral control," is a family of chronic neurobiological disorders. These neurobiological disorders affect our capacity to attend to tasks (inattention), inhibit behavior (impulsivity), and regulate activity level (hyperactivity) in developmentally appropriate ways. These impairments affect our capacity for planning, sequencing, problem solving, initiation of action, and self-control.

In recent years, thanks largely to major advances in neuroscience, our understanding of the underlying causes of ADD has grown exponentially. Perhaps most valuable is the growing awareness that ADD is not specific to one particular region of the brain. It is seen in dopamine depletions, abnormalities, and disregulation throughout the prefrontal, frontal, striatal, limbic, and basal ganglia regions of the brain. These five areas together are heavily involved in the control, planning, and execution of complex behaviors such as inhibition, arousal, attention, memory, planning, sequencing, and rhythm. They are also heavily involved in processing and reacting to sensory-motor input.

Running from Boredom

For almost anyone with ADD, there is an underlying and ever-present issue of whether an activity is boring or interesting. Dr. John Bailey, director of the Center for Attention & Learning in Mobile, Alabama, and member of on the Professional Advisory Board of ADDA, has said he considers a hallmark of ADD to be "the constant fleeing from boredom."

If something is interesting, it seems we could do it almost forever. When fully engaged, we often forget to eat and easily put off sleep, looking up from our efforts and finding to our surprise that it is dawn. If something is tedious, it is simply very difficult for a person with ADD to do. No matter the importance of the activity, if something is not sufficiently interesting to sustain our attention, if it is underwhelming, our brains can enter an underactive and disregulated state where we no longer feel alert and "alive."

In response to underwhelm, our sensory system goes on high alert to activate our underactive systems. When this happens, we find ourselves paying attention to absolutely everything. We may become fascinated by what's going on outside the window or the conversations of the people around us, or suddenly we may notice that our clothing is fitting uncomfortably or in some form of disarray. Or we might turn inward in our search for stimulation. We may start to ruminate on an ugly spat we just had with a family member, or get anxious about the long list of things we need to get done today. All of these are unconscious attempts on our part to stimulate our interest, to regain our comfort zone, to be at our optimal alertness level for the task at hand.

Unfortunately, without understanding why we are suddenly attracted to the view out the window or the other conversations in the room, we punish the very fidgetiness that is our natural and unconscious reaction to an understimulated brain. It is at this point we call our attractions distractions, which sadly we denigrate and make efforts to eliminate.

Fidgeting Effectively and Respectfully

Fidgets are any simultaneous sensory-motor stimulation strategy, easy to remember as the four S's. They are strategies for use in the moment. If something in which we are engaged is not interesting enough to sustain our focus, the additional sensory-motor input that is mildly stimulating, interesting, or entertaining, allows our brains to become fully engaged, and allows us to sustain focus on the primary activity at hand. We typically employ these strategies unconsciously, because at some level we know they help us to be in the appropriate state of mind.

Training ourselves to fidget effectively involves developing two of the most important skills we can ever learn: self-monitoring and self-regulation. The concept of being in an optimal alertness for a given situation is new to most of us, but as we begin to pay attention, we can experience the value of it. We need to be calm and alert for most desk tasks, able to sit still and focus on the work at hand. We need to be active and alert when we play sports, reacting quickly to outmaneuver our opponents. We need to be peaceful and drowsy to fall asleep. If our internal state and the requirements of our external activity are out of sync, it can be very difficult to function and behave in an appropriate and successful manner.

Once we understand this concept of optimal alertness, we can begin to train ourselves in self-monitoring. We can begin to notice when we're underwhelmed or over stimulated. Once we understand about our brain's need for a certain level of stimulation, and how our natural sensory-motor activities can provide just the right amount for a given situation, we can begin to train ourselves in self-regulation, using resources that are always available to us.

Part of learning to fidget effectively is learning to choose a fidget that not only works for us in that moment, but that is also situationally appropriate and respectful of those around us. In combining understanding of self-regulation with respectfulness to those around us, we also gain a much greater sense of self and self-respect.

The essence of *Fidget to Focus* is discovering the rhythm of our senses. It does not only exist in the most obvious of hyperactive children with a restless leg or a fidgety foot or even drumming fingers. Sensory fidgets are also found in more subtle environments for those with the Inattentive Type of ADD. Visual fidgets include glancing at things in the background, noticing falling leaves, watching cars passing by, or even observing the movement of fan blades overhead. Auditory fidgets may be the whispers in the crowd, the other conversations at a party, or the rhythmic beat of music in the background. Impulsivity is reflected in the rhythms of movement. There are even rhythms in our thoughts, day dreams, and emotional responses.

Once we recognize the cycle or rhythm of our senses, the challenge is to blend two or more senses to facilitate sustained focus. The selective rhythm of sensory movement is exercising for your brain. We fidget to focus. As we begin to honor and trust this rhythm, the dance of life changes to three steps forward and one step back.

What Next?

Fidgeting as a strategy to sustain focus is a short-term strategy for use in the moment. But what about strategies for long-term change? Fidget strategies can be applied whenever there is a need, but the shift in the brain's ability to focus is temporary. While there is little evidence yet of permanent change from persistent use of these simultaneous sensory stimulation strategies, there is mounting evidence to suggest that when the sensory inputs are repeated, regulated, and rehearsed, focus is achieved which may be generalized to other situations.

A recent book by Dr. John Ratey, professor of psychiatry at Harvard Medical School, is *A User's Guide to the Brain*. In it, Dr. Ratey presents, in lay person's terms, all that is known about the brain based on recent advances in the neurosciences. He lucidly explains how our new understanding of neurology fits in with what we already know from other fields of study such as psychology, anthropology, and linguistics. He introduces his readers to the concept of neuroplasticity, and that like our muscles, the more we exercise our brains, the better our brains work. These advances in neuroscience hold out hope that through appropriate exercises that stimulate the brain, we might be able to make not just momentary, but semi-permanent or even permanent improvements in brain function.

Currently, we see some evidence for such improvements through the use of neurofeedback training. Because of the nature of neurofeedback (or any biofeedback intervention for that matter), there have been no large double-blind population studies, the gold standard in medical science for determining whether or not something is an effective treatment. Yet there is evidence of success from many small clinical studies, at least within the time frame of the study, that people experience sustained focus after repetitive training on auditory and visual computer displays.

Another approach using biofeedback is the Interactive Metronome. This program challenges the person to synchronize a range of hand and foot motions to a precise reference tone. This intensive and repetitive training is thought to help develop, among other things, a more acute internal sense of timing (which is important in regulating all sorts of interactions), improve motor planning and sequencing, and help develop increased sustained attention.

The Dore Program, written about by Drs. Edward Hallowell and John Ratey in their latest book, *Delivered from Distraction*, is a program that uses specific physical exercises to develop and improve function of the cerebellum. Better functioning of the cerebellum leads to improved broad-ranging aspects of cognitive function including improvement in reading, writing, and comprehension, memory, concentration, and organizational skills.

Brain Gym, developed in 1981 by Dr. Paul and Gail Dennison, is a program based on a concept they developed called educational kinesiology, or enhanced learning through movement. The Dennisons believe these exercises stimulate and balance the brain's activities between left and right hemispheres, front and back regions, and the top and bottom parts of the brain. The exercises are designed to prepare the brain for, and then sustain, various cognitive activities.

And finally, we have learned of two activities that sound like fun and that intrigue us. The first, Drumstick Spinology™, is the simple and fantastic art of spinning drumsticks. The techniques are described in a book by the same name, available on the Internet, but what caught our attention is an associated article by Kurt Kuhn, DC, who writes about the value of this activity for permanently improving the focus of the children with whom he works. The second, Speed Stacks, is reported to be the fastest growing new sport in the country. The object is to stack and unstack twelve specially designed plastic cups in predetermined sequences, racing against the clock for fastest or best times. It has to be seen to be believed, but it clearly develops speed and bilateral coordination. The accompanying Web site (see appendices) states that this sport helps in many areas because "increasing bilateral proficiency (equal performance on both sides of the body) develops a greater percentage of the right side of the brain which houses awareness, focus, creativity and rhythm."

These are just some of the activities and programs we are aware of that have identified repetitive sensory-motor activities as a fundamental strategy for improving attention and other cognitive abilities. As advances in our sciences continue to increase our understanding and knowledge of our own biology over the coming years, we expect to see more innovative research and practices that teach us how to most effectively use sensory-motor strategies to develop and maintain better cognitive ability over time.

Finale

To live life with ADD is to anticipate and expect differences. It is the wonder of being creatively eccentric. To live life with ADD is to embrace the passion, notice the differences, expect the unexpected, and find the rhythm in the chaos. It is to fidget with attitude. Do it with respect for yourself and for others. We play our part in a much greater rhythm of life in which everybody plays their own key role. Welcome to the fraternity of those who *Fidget to Focus*.

Why do we fidget? Because we can!

APPENDIX 1

References

Amen, Daniel, M.D. Healing ADD: *The Breakthrough Program that Allows You to See and Heal the Six Types of ADD*. New York: Berkley Publishing Group, 2001.

_____. SPECT images of an ADD brain at rest and in concentration: brainplace.com/bp/atlas/ch12.asp

American Psychiatric Association. *Diagnostic and Statistical Manual of Mental Disorders*, 4th ed. Washington, DC: American Psychiatric Association, 1994.

American Psychiatric Association. *Diagnostic and Statistical Manual of Mental Disorders*, 3rd ed. Washington, DC: American Psychiatric Association, 1980.

American Psychiatric Association. *Diagnostic and Statistical Manual of Mental Disorders*, 2nd ed. Washington, DC: American Psychiatric Association, 1968.

Aron, Elaine N. *The Highly Sensitive Person: How to Thrive when the World Overwhelms You*. New York: Random House, 1996.

Ayres, A. Jean. *Sensory Integration and the Child.* Los Angeles: Western Psychological Services, 1979.

Barkley, Russell, Ph.D. "ADHD/ADD: An Intensive Course on the Nature and Treatment of Children and Adolescents with Attention Deficit Hyperactivity Disorder," Relationship Training Institute, February 6, 2004.

Brain Gym. www.braingym.com

Dore Achievement Centers. www.dorecenters.com

Hallowell, Edward M., M.D. and Ratey, John J., M.D. *Delivered from Distraction: Getting the Most out of Life with Attention Deficit Disorder.* New York: Random House. 2005.

_____. *Driven to Distraction: Recognizing and Coping with Attention Deficit Disorder from Childhood through Adulthood.* New York: Random House, 1994.

Hartmann, Thom, et al. *Thom Hartmann's Compete Guide to ADHD: Help for Your Family at Home, School, and Work.* Grass Valley, CA: Underwood Books, 2000.

Heller, Sharon. *Too Loud, Too Bright, Too Fast, Too Tight: What to Do if You Are Sensory Defensive in an Overstimulating World.* New York: HarperCollins, 2002.

Horacek, H. Joseph Jr. *Brainstorms: Understanding and Treating the Emotional Storms of Attention Deficit Hyperactivity Disorder*

from Childhood Through Adulthood. Northvale, NJ: Jason Aaronson Inc., 1998.

Interactive Metronome. www.interactivemetronome.com

Jones, Clare B., Ph.D. *Sourcebook for Children With Attention Deficit Disorder: A Management Guide for Early Childhood Professionals and Parents.* San Antonio, TX: Communication Skill Builders, A Division of The Psychological Corporation, 1991.

Kranowitz, Carol Stock. *The Out-Of-Sync Child: Recognizing and Coping with Sensory Integration Dysfunction.* New York: Skylight Press, 1998.

Kuhn, Kurt. (2002) "Healthystix for Your Brain." https://www.htmlmanager.net/userpages/roger/spinology.html

Ratey, John, M.D. "A User's Guide to the Brain." The Connection. http://archives.theconnection.org/archive/2001/02/0202a.shtml

_____. *A User's Guide to the Brain: Perception, Attention, and the Four Theaters of the Brain.* New York: Vintage, 2001.

_____, and Miller, Andrea. "Foibles, Frailties, and Frustrations Seen through the Lens of Attention," *Challenge,* January/February 1992.

Speed Stacks. www.speedstacks.com

Strong, Jeff (1998) "Rhythmic Entrainment Intervention: A Theoretical Perspective." www.reiinstitute.com

Thompson, L. "Complementary Therapeutic Interventions: Neurofeedback, Metacognition, and Nutrition for Long-Term Improvement In Attention Deficit Hyperactivity Disorder," pp. 405-407 in *Therapist's Guide to Learning and Attention Disorders*. Fine, Aubrey H. and Kotkin, Ronald A., eds. San Diego: Elsevier Science, 2003.

Trott, Maryann Colby, with Laurel, Marci, and Windeck, Susan. *SenseAbilities: Understanding Sensory Integration*. Tucson, AZ: Therapy Skill Builders, 1993.

Vitale, Barbara Meister. *Unicorns Are Real: A Right-Brained Approach to Learning*. New York: Jalmar Press, 1982.

Walters, Dottie. *Speak and Grow Rich, Revised and Expanded*. Prentice Hall, 1997.

Wilkinson L., Scholey A., Wesnes K. "Chewing Gum Selectively Improves Aspects of Memory in Healthy Volunteers," *Appetite* 48, no. 3 (2002): 235-36.

Williams, Mary Sue, and Shellenberger, Sherry. *How Does Your Engine Run? A Leader's Guide To The Alert Program™ For Self-Regulation*. Albuquerque: Therapy Works, 1998.

Zametkin, A., Mordahl, T.E., Gross, M., King, A.C., Semple, W.E., Rumsey, J., Hamburger, S., & Cohen, R.M. "Cerebral Glucose Metabolism in Adults with Hyperactivity of Childhood Onset." *New England Journal of Medicine* 323 (1990): 1361-1366.

APPENDIX 2

Resources

Web Sites with Information on ADD

There are many sites on the Web with information about ADD. Many are promoting products or specific agendas. The links listed here are to nonprofit organizations whose primary goal is to provide the best possible information on ADD and related topics.

ADDA: Attention Deficit Disorder Association
www.add.org

CHADD: Children & Adults with ADHD
www.chadd.org

CHADD's National Resource Center on ADHD
www.help4adhd.org

National Center for Gender Issues and ADD
www.ncgiadd.org

ADD Resources. A very rich site with lots of links.
www.addresources.org

An ADD/ADHD site based in England
www.ADDers.org

Born to Explore! The other side of ADD
www.borntoexplore.org

National Institute of Mental Health
www.nimh.nih.gov

Learning Disabilities Association of America
www.ldanatl.org

Magazines and Newsletters with Information on ADD

There are some great magazines and newsletters for those with ADD. The following are home sites for some of them, all of which are helpful and informative Web sites in their own right.

ADDitude **Magazine**
www.ADDitudeMag.com

Attention! **Magazine, comes with membership to CHADD**
www.CHADD.org

Focus **Magazine, comes with membership to ADDA**
www.ADD.org

About Attention Deficit Disorder, **E-mail Newsletter.**
From Eileen Bailey. Lots of information and links to other sites.
Keeps up-to-date with the latest news in the ADD world.
www.add.about.com

ADD ADHD Advances, **E-mail Newsletter**
From Dr. Anthony Kane. Information on conventional and
alternative treatment options.
www.addadhdadvances.com

ADDvance, **E-mail Newsletter**
From Drs. Patricia Quinn and Kathleen Nadeau. A site dedicated to the needs of women and girls with ADD.
www.ADDvance.com

ADHDnews, **E-mail Newsletter**
From Brandi Valentine. Started in 1995. Lots of information that
is continually updated.
www.ADHDnews.com

All Kinds of Minds, **E-mail Newsletter**
From Dr. Mel Levine. Resources and information about learning
disabilities.
www.allkindsofminds.org

Products for ADD

These sites have additional information as well as products for
sale that may be of interest to people with ADD.

ADD Consults
The first and only virtual online ADD clinic. Includes articles, resources, an ADD store (good source of fidgets), online support groups, private, personal ADD consultations by e-mail, and more.
www.addconsults.com

ADHD.com
This site is maintained by Eli Lilly and Company, makers of Strattera, a drug used to treat ADD.
www.adhd.com

The ADD Information Library
This is a very informative site, affiliated with a dietary supplement called Attend, marketed as a homeopathic "alternative to Ritalin" by Växa Homeopathic Medicinals. This site also offers an e-mail newsletter.
www.newideas.net

ADD Support Company
This Web site is maintained by Shire US Inc., makers of Adderall XR, a drug used to treat ADD.
www.adhdsupportcompany.com

A.D.D. Warehouse
An extensive collection of ADD-related books, videos, training programs, games, professional texts and assessment products.
www.addwarehouse.com

Focus on ADD
This Web site is maintained by McNeil Pharmaceuticals, makers of Concerta, a drug used to treat ADD.
www.focusonadhd.com

Sensory-Motor Programs for Cognitive Effectiveness

These programs, activities, and organizations all use or promote the use of various sensory-motor activities to increase cognitive effectiveness.

The Alert Program
From the site: "An innovative program for children, teachers, parents, and therapists that uses sensory-based strategies to help individuals reach and maintain optimal alertness."
www.alertprogram.com

Brain Gym, Edu-Kinesthetics, Inc.
From the site: "Developmental experts have known for more than eighty years that movement enhances learning. Beginning in the 1970s, educator and reading specialist Paul E. Dennison, Ph.D., researched these movements, simplified them, and created techniques to make them effective for everyone, developing a whole new way of understanding the learning process."
www.braingym.com

DORE Achievement Centers
From the site: "The Dore exercise program directly addresses the physiological source of your problem. Our exercises are individualized. They stimulate the cerebellum, a part of the brain shown to be integrally involved in learning and attention. The results typically include improved ability to learn (e.g. mental processing, concentration, and memory) as well as increased confidence and physical coordination."
www.dorecenters.com

Drumstick Spinology™
From the site: "The first book ever written and devoted to the subject of spinning (twirling) drumsticks: 'Healthystix' for Your Brain."
https://www.htmlmanager.net/userpages/roger/spinology.html

Fast ForWord®
From the site: "The Fast ForWord family of products use neuroscience principles to create an optimal learning environment that enables you to:
Simultaneously develop multiple skill sets to maximize learning;
Identify reading and language difficulties;
Attack the underlying causes of these difficulties."
www.scilearn.com

Interactive Metronome
From the site: "The IM program provides a structured, goal-oriented process that challenges the patient to synchronize a range of hand and foot exercises to a precise computer-generated reference tone heard through headphones. The patient attempts to match the rhythmic beat with repetitive motor actions. Over the course of the treatment, patients learn to: focus and attend for longer periods of time, increase physical endurance and stamina, filter out internal and external distractions, improve ability to monitor mental and physical actions as they are occurring, and progressively improve performance."
www.interactivemetronome.com

Journey to Wild Divine
From the site: "The Journey to Wild Divine is the first 'inner-active' computer adventure that combines ancient breathing and

meditation with modern biofeedback technology for total mind-body wellness."
www.wilddivine.com

Play Attention
From the site: "The Play Attention Learning System is a patented advance of technology NASA astronauts and U.S. Air Force pilots use to stay attentive in the cockpit. Now you can use this same technology in your home and Use Your Head® to overcome attention, concentration and focus issues."
www.playattention.com

Rhythmic Entrainment Institute
Generic and custom CDs developed around variations of rhythmic drumming that facilitate focus, relaxation, and/or well-being.
www.reiinstitute.com

Society for Auditory Intervention Techniques
From the site: "The Society for Auditory Intervention Techniques (SAIT) distributes information about auditory integration training (AIT) and other auditory-based interventions to professionals and parents."
www.sait.org

Speed Stacks, Inc.
From the site: "Cup stacking is now the fastest growing new sport in the country. Participants stack and unstack twelve specially designed plastic cups in pre-determined sequences. Stackers race against the clock for fastest or best times. Stackers also compete on a relay team racing against another team in head-to-head competition. Increasing bilateral proficiency (equal performance on both sides of the body) develops a greater

percentage of the right side of the brain, which houses awareness, focus, creativity and rhythm."
www.speedstacks.com

Sensory-Motor Resources

Most of these resources are aimed at occupational therapy and children's needs. Many of the resources are suitable for adults as well. There are a number of great fidgets available at these sites.

Achievement Products for Children
From the site: "Hundreds of top-quality therapy, exercise, and special education products to help children achieve their best."
www.specialkidszone.com

Heads Up!
Several pages with fidgets and other products for help with ADD.
www.headsupnow.com

Sensory Comfort
From the site: "Products for children and adults who have sensory processing differences." White noise machines, Disc-o-sits, and much more.
www.sensorycomfort.com

Theraproducts
The best and most extensive source of fidgets and occupational therapy products aimed at children that we know of.
www.theraproducts.com

Therapy Shoppe

From the site: "Extraordinary little specialty shoppe for school and pediatric therapists, teachers, and parents too." Lots of good stuff.
www.therapyshoppe.com

Therapy Toy Shop

Another extensive collection of therapeutic equipment, books, toys, and games.
www.therapytoyshop.com

Fidgets for Grown-Ups

These are sites with fidgets and fun stuff for grown-ups.

ADD Consults

The first and only virtual online ADD clinic. Includes an online store with a selection of fidgets.
www.addconsults.com

Micro Egg Timer

From the site: "This unique little timer can help you not to forget the world around you while sitting at the PC. It has a simple and friendly user interface and can be set with just a couple of mouse clicks or keystrokes."
www.mic-ro.com/eggtimer

The Orb Factory

From the site: "The Orb Factory Ltd. is a Canadian designer and manufacturer of innovative toys, craft kits, puzzles, and educational products. Our mandate is to offer our customers a clear

alternative to existing toy offerings through the quality of our designs, the play value, and educational content of our products."
www.orbfactory.com

Star Magic Space Age Gifts
The coolest source of fidget toys for adults that we know of. Be sure to check out the "Executive Toys" section!
www.starmagic.com

Trainers Warehouse
The "Toys for Learners" section of this site also has good fidgets.
www.trainerswarehouse.com

APPENDIX 3

Fidget Strategies Workbook

Introduction

Fidgets are simultaneous sensory-motor stimulation strategies-the four S's. If something we are engaged in is not interesting enough to sustain our focus, the additional sensory-motor input that is mildly stimulating, interesting, or entertaining allows our brains to become fully engaged and allows us to sustain focus on the primary activity in which we are participating. The strategy we choose should not employ the same sense or modality we are using for the primary activity, or it will divert rather than support our attention and focus. Additionally, part of learning to fidget effectively is learning to choose a fidget that not only works for us in that moment, but that is also situationally appropriate and respectful of those around us.

In this appendix, we list small, subtle tricks or fidgets that many people use consciously or unconsciously to remain alert and focused on activities that otherwise may seem too tedious in that moment. These lists have been compiled from years of listening to clients, patients, and support group members. We offer these tricks not as a definitive list, but as grist for the mill to help you figure out what works best for you.

If you find a strategy that isn't listed here, we hope you will share it with us via our Web site: www.FidgettoFocus.com. We know you will have your own interesting stories to tell, and we look forward to hearing from you!

Instructions

To most effectively use these lists, we suggest that you treat this appendix like a workbook. We have provided the following guidelines to help you make the most of these lists, but they are of course just suggestions. We know ADD, and we expect you to "color outside the lines"!

First, identify one activity that you have trouble attending to and for which you would like to find an effective fidget or menu of fidgets.

Second, if applicable, identify the primary sensory mechanism(s) required for that activity.

Third, make note of what you already do to sustain your focus when you engage in that activity. Use the checklists for this, marking off ones that work for you and adding new ones as you discover them.

Fourth, using both the checklists and your existing strategies as inspiration, experiment with new strategies to see what works best for you in that moment when the activity is just not interesting enough to sustain your attention.

Finally, you may want to write down your ideas and results. One aspect of living with ADD is that we forget to do what we know. In addition to writing down what you learn about yourself and what fidgets work for you, it might be a good idea to return to this section from time to time to review and remind yourself of possible strategies.

Fidget Strategies by Modality

In this approach to effective fidgeting, we have made lists of fidgets by modality, or sensory-motor activity. They represent the distilled accumulated experience of hundreds of people who have shared their stories with us.

Before proceeding, remember that different tasks require different strategies. First choose one activity or task for which to develop strategies:

- ❑ reading
- ❑ writing
- ❑ conversations
- ❑ lectures
- ❑ meetings
- ❑ driving
- ❑ exercising
- ❑ watching television
- ❑ housework or other physical chore
- ❑ paperwork or other desk-type chore
- ❑ falling asleep
- ❑ other _____

Now remember, the best fidget strategies will use a different modality than the primary one required for the task. Choose the primary sensory-motor activity required for this task:

❑ seeing
❑ hearing
❑ tasting
❑ smelling
❑ using one's mouth
❑ using one's hands-fine motor activity
❑ using one's body-gross motor activity
❑ other _____

Finally, go through the following lists of strategies and identify the ones you already use when doing this particular boring or monotonous task (check all that apply):

Sight

These strategies involve noticing details in the environment or watching, noticing, or tracking something while engaged in the mundane task. They also involve setting up our environments with elements that support successful visual fidgeting.

❑ selecting colorful furnishings, walls, etc.
❑ creating a decorated desk or work area
❑ maintaining an active and organized work area
❑ using colorful tools (e.g., pens, folders, highlighters)
❑ using adjustable lighting
❑ watching a fish tank, water/oil toy, screen saver, etc.

- ❑ watching flickering flames/fireplace
- ❑ glancing out a window
- ❑ scanning TV shows, channel surfing
- ❑ playing video/computer games
- ❑ other _____

Sound

These strategies involve listening to or hearing something while reading, talking, planning, etc.

- ❑ playing familiar music (e.g., classical, rock, jazz)
- ❑ listening to pulsating, rhythmic beats
- ❑ whistling or humming to yourself
- ❑ talking to yourself
- ❑ listening to television or talk radio
- ❑ listening to a ticking clock or timer
- ❑ hearing background noise (conversations, traffic, etc.)
- ❑ playing white noise
- ❑ other _____

Movement

These strategies involve wiggling, moving, or doing something while listening, studying, talking, etc.

- ❑ swiveling in a desk chair
- ❑ balancing a chair on two legs
- ❑ rearranging the objects on your desk
- ❑ rocking, fidgeting, or squirming

- ❏ swinging or bouncing foot or leg
- ❏ wiggling toes
- ❏ drumming or tapping fingers or pen
- ❏ cracking knuckles
- ❏ tensing, then relaxing individual muscles
- ❏ rolling head and neck back and forth
- ❏ stretching or flexing or shaking body
- ❏ taking a deep breath
- ❏ standing
- ❏ pacing back and forth or in circles
- ❏ walking
- ❏ driving a car, motorcycle, boat, etc.
- ❏ exercising (e.g., cycling, jogging)
- ❏ dancing
- ❏ other _____

Touch

These strategies primarily involve sensations in the hands, not just movement. For instance, holding, feeling, or handling something while watching, listening, talking, etc.

- ❏ stroking or petting animals
- ❏ stroking or touching your face
- ❏ tapping or drumming fingers
- ❏ fidget toys (balls, Silly Putty, Slinky, etc.)
- ❏ folding, tearing, or otherwise playing with paper
- ❏ twisting, stroking, or playing with hair

- ❑ clicking a pen or mechanical pencil
- ❑ twisting phone cord, necklace, watch, etc.
- ❑ rubbing or stroking a cuff, hem, or wrinkle ("silkies")
- ❑ shuffling or manipulating cards or a coin (magic tricks)
- ❑ fiddling or fidgeting with keys or coins
- ❑ jingling items in pocket
- ❑ taking notes
- ❑ doodling
- ❑ painting, sketching, drawing
- ❑ whittling
- ❑ knitting or crocheting (or doing other needlework)
- ❑ other _____

Mouth

These specialized combinations of touch and movement strategies typically involve putting something in the mouth while reading, working, etc.

- ❑ biting or chewing on pens, pencils, gum, ice
- ❑ chewing on sleeves, cuffs, sweatshirt strings
- ❑ licking, sucking, or biting your lips/cheeks/tongue
- ❑ biting nails or cuticles
- ❑ snacking on chips, veggies, sweets
- ❑ sipping coffee, soda, water
- ❑ sucking on candy, ice
- ❑ chewing gum
- ❑ clenching jaw, grinding teeth

❑ whistling

❑ smoking

❑ other _____

Taste

These strategies involve the use of flavors, textures, and temperatures of food and drink rather than the chewing, sipping, sucking, or blowing of the mouth strategies listed above. These all involve putting something in the mouth while reading, listening, working, etc.

❑ eating or licking salty, sour, savory, or sweet flavors

❑ eating crunchy or chewy snacks

❑ drinking hot tea, coffee, or cocoa

❑ drinking iced water or carbonated drink

❑ strong flavors such as mint, lemon, cinnamon, or ginger

❑ eating foods seasoned with hot peppers, curries

❑ other _____

Smell

These strategies are far less commonly recognized and used than the strategies listed above. Because our sense of smell is directly linked to our emotional centers, smell strategies often evoke emotional responses, which are themselves stimulation strategies.

❑ scented markers or pens

❑ scented candles

❑ fresh, crisp air

- ❏ incense
- ❏ aromatherapy
- ❏ cleaning products (e.g., ammonia, bleach, lemon oil)
- ❏ dinner on the stove
- ❏ cinnamon rolls at the bakery
- ❏ popcorn at the theater
- ❏ other _____

Time

The following strategies help develop a sense of time. This sense, which is notoriously bad in people with ADD, is a central feature in the disregulation of exective functions.

- ❏ racing—beat the clock or another person
- ❏ sprinting—do as much as possible in a short period
- ❏ divide and conquer—pick one piece to accomplish now
- ❏ rewards—take a break or move to another activity
- ❏ accountability—create self-imposed consequences or involve another person

Fidget Strategies by Activity

This is an alternative approach to finding fidgets to help sustain attention while engaged in less than engrossing activities. Here we emphasize environmental factors that affect our stimulation levels, as well as specific individual fidgets that may be supported by the environment we choose or that are completely independent of it. There are often multiple ways we can tailor our environment or employ sensory-motor activities to help us be comfortably in the right zone for any given activity.

At the beginning of the "Fidget Strategies by Modality" section, we noted almost a dozen different kinds of tasks that might not prove interesting enough to sustain our attention. Rather than going through each of these activities individually, we will provide a few examples to illustrate how to identify strategies that might make staying focused on these tasks easier. We have chosen three types of activities as examples: the strategies that might help with a sit-down task such as reading or writing, the strategies that might help with an active task such as chores, and the strategies that might help with falling asleep. We hope these lists and workbook approach will help you to determine the best strategies for you.

If you find a strategy that isn't listed here, we hope you will share it with us via our Web site. We know you will have your own interesting stories to tell, and we look forward to hearing from you!

Strategies for Reading or Writing

To identify which fidgets and environments work best to help you sustain your attention while you are reading or writing, try answering these questions:

Specify the reading or writing task

Reading:

❑ newspaper

❑ magazine

❑ recreational

- ❑ informational
- ❑ textbook
- ❑ other _____

Writing:

- ❑ letter
- ❑ journal
- ❑ homework assignment
- ❑ research paper
- ❑ newsletter
- ❑ book
- ❑ other _____

Which medium is the easiest for you or the most fun?
Reading:

- ❑ conventional print book
- ❑ e-book
- ❑ audio-book
- ❑ having someone read to you
- ❑ other _____

Writing:

- ❑ loose-leaf paper
- ❑ bound composition book or journal
- ❑ spiral-bound notebook
- ❑ computer
- ❑ dictation
- ❑ other _____

if applicable:

- ❏ what kind, size, and color of paper?
- ❏ what kind of rule (lined, unlined, graph)?
- ❏ what kind of writing implement (pen, pencil, marker)?

Which venue works best for this quiet activity?

- ❏ public or school library
- ❏ coffeehouse
- ❏ outdoors, perhaps in a park
- ❏ office
- ❏ bedroom
- ❏ kitchen table
- ❏ living room or den
- ❏ bathroom
- ❏ totally alone
- ❏ with another person who is also working quietly
- ❏ other _____

Which time of day works best for this quiet activity?

- ❏ predawn
- ❏ early morning
- ❏ late morning
- ❏ lunch break
- ❏ afternoon
- ❏ night
- ❏ after midnight
- ❏ other _____

Which lighting environment works best for this activity?

- ❏ incandescent
- ❏ fluorescent
- ❏ natural
- ❏ bright light
- ❏ subdued light
- ❏ in between

Which seating strategies help with this quiet activity?

- ❏ hard, like a ladder-backed wooden chair
- ❏ soft, like a padded armchair
- ❏ rocking chair
- ❏ swivel chair
- ❏ desk chair
- ❏ beanbag chair
- ❏ other _____

Try sitting on an exercise ball and see how that affects your ability to concentrate. What about the floor? Or the couch? Or the bed? Or the bathtub?

Which movement strategies help with this quiet activity?

- ❏ standing
- ❏ swaying
- ❏ walking
- ❏ rocking
- ❏ bouncing
- ❏ wiggling part of your body

❏ fiddling with or stroking something

❏ other _____

Which sound strategies help with this quiet activity?

❏ quiet

❏ loud music

❏ soft music

❏ talking to yourself

❏ television or talk radio in the background

❏ white noise, like the hum of a fan or humidifier

❏ other _____

Which mouth or taste strategies help with this activity?

This is a short list of mouth and taste strategies. For additional ideas, you might want to review the lists in the "Fidget Strategies by Modality" section at the beginning of this appendix.

❏ chewing gum

❏ sucking on candy or ice

❏ tasting strong flavors such as mint, lemon, cinnamon, or ginger

❏ clenching jaw, grinding teeth

❏ whistling

❏ smoking

❏ other _____

Which time strategies work for this quiet activity?

❏ short sprints

❏ working until a specified amount has been done

- ❏ divide and conquer—pick one piece to accomplish now
- ❏ planned breaks
- ❏ rewards for specific accomplishments
- ❏ consequences
- ❏ other _____

Strategies for Falling Asleep

As we noted earlier, falling asleep is a struggle for many people with ADD. We can have a hard time letting go of the day; our minds race and we cannot settle down. We may be too bored to fall asleep. Or, we simply may not feel sleepy when it's time to go to bed. Try observing your current strategies, and try some new ones based on these ideas from others with ADD.

Which venue works best for you to fall asleep?
- ❏ bed
- ❏ bunk
- ❏ couch
- ❏ hammock
- ❏ floor

also (check and/or circle each one that applies)
- ❏ small or large space
- ❏ high or low ceiling
- ❏ familiar or novel location
- ❏ window open or closed
- ❏ door open or closed
- ❏ other _____

Which time of day works best for you to fall asleep?

Some of us fall asleep easily, but at a later hour than most others. Some of us find we have a window of opportunity in which we can fall asleep easily. For some of us, there is no pattern. What about you?

Which lighting environments help you fall asleep?

- ❏ total dark
- ❏ night-light
- ❏ lamplight
- ❏ ambient light from windows
- ❏ flicker of television
- ❏ other _____

Which touch strategies help you fall asleep?

(check and circle those that apply)

- ❏ hard bed or soft
- ❏ heavy blankets or light
- ❏ tightly tucked in or loose-fitting bedclothes
- ❏ silky or fuzzy textures in blankets or night clothes
- ❏ teddy bear, sleeping partner, or alone
- ❏ room cool or warm
- ❏ air circulating or still
- ❏ other _____

Which movements help you fall asleep?

- ❏ clenching and relaxing one muscle at a time
- ❏ holding an arm straight up in the air

- ❑ rocking your head back and forth
- ❑ deep breathing
- ❑ other _____

Which sounds help you fall asleep?

- ❑ perfect quiet
- ❑ white noise, perhaps from a fan or special audiotape
- ❑ music
- ❑ radio
- ❑ television
- ❑ ambient sounds from outside
- ❑ other _____

Which smells help you fall asleep?

- ❑ fresh air
- ❑ freshly washed sheets
- ❑ aromatherapy, for example, lavender oil
- ❑ other _____

Other strategies to help you fall asleep

These are strategies that that do not fall into one of the above categories. Several have to do with what you are thinking or imagining as you fall asleep. Others have to do with preparation for sleep.

- ❑ reading something interesting, but not too interesting
- ❑ watching television that is mildly entertaining
- ❑ guided imagery, either self-guided or from a tape
- ❑ meditation

❑ a hot bath before bed

❑ a glass of warm milk before bed

Strategies for Doing Chores

Staying on top of chores is not easily compatible with having ADD. Chores are typically boring and you can never be rid of them. Every day there are chores to do, and if they are not done regularly, they turn into ugly monsters that you really do not want to deal with. Probably the best strategy is to have someone else do them for you, or at least to have another person do them with you. Company helps keep the time spent doing the chores more fun, and it shortens the time required to do the chores, another plus. Unfortunately, having help is not always an option. When you are stuck doing the chores yourself, try some of these strategies and see what happens.

Which chore?

❑ doing laundry (washing, drying, ironing, putting away)

❑ sorting mail (bills, letters, notices, catalogues, junk)

❑ paying bills

❑ shopping for groceries

❑ making meals

❑ doing dishes

❑ cleaning house

❑ doing yard work

❑ other _____

Which time of day and day of the week works best to do this chore?

- ❏ predawn
- ❏ early morning
- ❏ late morning
- ❏ lunch break
- ❏ afternoon
- ❏ night
- ❏ after midnight
- ❏ Monday
- ❏ Tuesday
- ❏ Wednesday
- ❏ Thursday
- ❏ Friday
- ❏ Saturday
- ❏ Sunday

Which sound strategies help with this chore?

- ❏ playing music (what kind of music? loud or soft?)
- ❏ listening to pulsating, rhythmic beats
- ❏ whistling or humming to yourself
- ❏ talking to yourself
- ❏ listening to television or talk radio
- ❏ listening to a ticking clock or timer
- ❏ playing white noise in the background
- ❏ other _____

Which mouth or taste strategies work for this chore?

For additional ideas beyond this short list, you might want to review the lists in the "Fidget Strategies by Modality" section at the beginning of this appendix.

- ❑ chewing gum
- ❑ sucking on candy or ice
- ❑ tasting strong flavors such as mint, lemon, cinnamon, or ginger
- ❑ clenching jaw, grinding teeth
- ❑ whistling
- ❑ smoking
- ❑ other _____

Which time strategies work for this chore?

- ❑ racing—beat the clock or another person
- ❑ sprinting—do as much as possible in a short period
- ❑ divide and conquer—pick one piece to accomplish now
- ❑ working until a specified amount has been done
- ❑ planned breaks
- ❑ rewards
- ❑ consequences—self-imposed or involving another person
- ❑ other _____

Notes

Make note of what worked and what didn't. Create a menu of strategies for use with a given activity. Remember, things change and variety is one of the best ways to keep things interesting.

What works now might not work so well in the future. If that happens, you can come back to this exercise and find new or updated strategies to help you.

APPENDIX 4

About the Authors

Roland Rotz, Ph.D., is a licensed child and adult psychologist, director of the Lifespan Development Center in Carpinteria, California, and a nationally recognized expert on ADD. While offering a full range of diagnostic and clinical services, Dr. Rotz also specializes in the diagnosis and treatment of ADD and co-occurring conditions. Over the past 15 years, he has focused his attention on establishing and maintaining effective treatment strategies for children, adolescents, and adults with ADD. More recently, he has addressed the needs of those with chronic disorganization. Over the years, Dr. Rotz has begun and continues to facilitate support groups for adults in Santa Barbara, California. He is currently affiliated with the University of California, Santa Barbara and Santa Barbara City College. As an expert in the field of ADD, Dr. Rotz gives presentations regionally and nationally. You can visit his Web site: www.docrotz.com

Sarah Wright, M.S., A.C.T., is a professional personal coach, one of the few in the nation trained specifically to work with people affected by ADD. Sarah has also been a professional organizer, program manager, resource director, and corporate executive. Additionally, she is the parent of a child with ADD and Asperger's Syndrome, and knows first hand the joys and frustrations of living with these differences. She lives near San Diego, California, where in addition to her coaching, she is involved in ADD support groups, education, and advocacy. You can visit her Web site at: www.swcc.biz

APPENDIX 5

Contact the Authors

This book could not have been written without the stories shared by so many of you about the strategies that get you through the day. Yet this book will be the first time many readers have ever encountered such ideas. After all, it is so contrary to all that we have been taught, so counterintuitive to be able to pay better attention while doing two things at once. Yet we know it works. We know it works because so many people tell us so.

We are sure that as you read this book, it elicited many "aha" moments for you and awakened memories of your own experiences. We hope you will share them with us because we are also sure there are more stories out there, stories about strategies that are longtime allies for some, but that for others are new and desperately needed.

Whether you want to share what works for you, an ADD anecdote, or some expression of what fidgeting or underwhelm is like for you, please contact us through our Web site: www.FidgettoFocus.com

We look forward to hearing from you!

Roland Rotz
Sarah D. Wright
May 2005

APPENDIX 6

Final Thought

The Empty White Room
By Becky Wright, age 12

Boredom is like an empty room,
all white, and the only windows are too high to see out of,
and slowly, you start to go crazy.

You don't care anymore what you do
you just have to do SOMETHING
everything is empty white nothingness like a deep and endless
crevasse
but your mind is going wild
colors are exploding
everywhere
like fireworks
and
your thoughts
are darting everywhere
like a
hyper
fish,

not
caring
about what it is doing
but having
to let out
all
that
energy!

Then, in desperation, you notice the windows above you.
You know that you really really want to get out.
And you know the only way you can reach those windows
is by making a ladder of self-discipline, one rung at a time.
You know it will be hard, but it's the only way.
And finally, there is Hope.